SC 5/13

Using the environment 3 Tackling problems Part 1

A Unit for teachers

Published for the Schools Council by
Macdonald Educational, London and Milwaukee

First published in Great Britain 1974 by
Macdonald & Co (Publishers) Ltd
Maxwell House, Worship St
London EC2A 2EN

Macdonald-Raintree Inc.
205 W. Highland Avenue
Milwaukee, Wisconsin 53203

Reprinted 1977, 1980 (with amendments),
1982

ISBN 0 356 04356 8

Library of Congress Catalog Card Number
77-81802

The author of this book is:

Margaret Collis

The other members of the Science 5/13 team are:

Len Ennever	Project Director
Albert James	Deputy Project Director
Wynne Harlen	Evaluator

Don Radford
Roy Richards
Sheila Parker
Mary Horn

Made and printed by Waterlow Ltd., Dunstable

The Science 5/13 Project

'Science 5/13' is a project sponsored jointly by the Schools Council, the Nuffield Foundation and the Scottish Education Department, and based at the University of Bristol School of Education. It aims at helping teachers to help children between the ages of five and thirteen years to learn science through first-hand experience using a variety of methods.

The Project produces books that comprise Units dealing with subject areas in which children are likely to conduct investigations. Some of these Units are supported by books of background information. The Units are linked by objectives that the Project team hopes children will attain through their work. The aims of the Project are explained in a general guide for teachers called *With objectives in mind,* which contains the Project's guide to Objectives for children learning science, reprinted at the back of each Unit.

Foreword

Margaret Collis has been a valued friend of the Science 5/13 Project since it began. It is entirely appropriate, therefore, that having written *Using the environment,* she should, with characteristic generosity, have made it part of the Project's materials.

For years before the Project even began she, I and others in the Project team had been working together on teachers' courses and on committees of various kinds, exploring child-centred ways of working in science and helping to introduce them into schools. Margaret Collis still works tirelessly with teachers of varied experience, and in the generous atmosphere she always creates, they respond with enthusiasm and conviction. She has become aware of their doubts and uncertainties, and having accumulated a great store of first-hand knowledge about what they really want to know, she offers them the advice they need and through it the confidence they seek.

Both knowledge and advice are now recorded in a book for teachers to keep by them and to consult year by year. It took many years to write, and it will be many more in active service.

L. F. Ennever
University of Bristol
1974

Acknowledgements

The Project is deeply grateful to its many friends: to the local education authorities who have helped us work in their areas, to those of their staff who, acting as area representatives, have borne the heavy brunt of administering our trials, and to the teachers, heads and wardens who have been generous without stint in working with their children on our materials. The books we have written drew substance from the work they did for us, and it was through their critical appraisal that our materials reached their present form. For guidance, we had our sponsors, our Consultative Committee and, for support, in all our working, the University of Bristol. To all of them we acknowledge our many debts: their help has been invaluable.

It is a pleasure to acknowledge some further help of special value. Mr L. C. Comber, chairman of the Consultative Committee for the Science 5/13 Project and formerly HM Staff Inspector for Rural Studies, read the first draft of *Using the environment*. His comments and suggestions have been of the greatest possible assistance in the work that followed.

Some of the apparatus photographed in Volume 3 has been constructed by Mr W. A. J. Edwards and Mr D. Postill, Kent Education Committee Inspectors. They have also checked sections in this book where there is emphasis on mathematical ideas and the use of electricity.

Metrication

This has given us a great deal to think about. We have been given much good advice by well-informed friends, and we have consulted many reports by learned bodies. Following the advice and the reports whenever possible we have expressed quantities in metric units with Imperial units afterwards in square brackets if it seemed useful to state them so.

There are, however, some cases to which the recommendations are difficult to apply. For instance we have difficulty with units such as miles per hour (which has statutory force in this country) and with Imperial units that are still in current use for common commodities and, as far as we know, liable to remain so for some time. In these cases we have tried to use our common sense and, in order to make statements that are both accurate and helpful to teachers, we have quoted Imperial measures followed by the appropriate metric equivalents in square brackets if it seemed sensible to give them.

Where we have quoted statements made by children, or given illustrations that are children's work, we have left unaltered the units in which the children worked—in any case some of these units were arbitrary.

Contents

Introduction

This is a book about field studies. It deals with investigations and problems children can discover through their natural interest in their outdoor surroundings. Such first-hand experience, gained from the environment, is the basis of learning, provoking thought, giving children many ideas to share through speech and writing and sending them to books and other secondary sources of information to add to their own findings.

In the countryside there is so much more material of educational value than one book can cover that here there must be selection. We concern ourselves with things that have always interested scientists—natural phenomena that can be investigated through the human senses.

No rigid course with the same material for all is offered, that would fail to satisfy children's individual needs. When children work naturally they respond to the same starting points in different ways and soon become interested in different aspects of a common study. Later, as their development continues, they acquire the ability to make general statements about their experience or, as we usually say, 'form concepts', but, here again, it is through varied experience that each child's understanding of ideas is consolidated and deepened.

Piaget, and others, have shown that children pass through the same stages of intellectual development in acquiring the power of conceptual thought, but there is nothing sudden about this maturing, it is something children come to at their own rate with frequent returns to earlier ways of thinking and working when new situations have to be faced. This means that we shall find children, even of the same age, at different stages in the way they learn from their surroundings, so teachers must be prepared to vary their influence correspondingly. For these reasons the material in this book is arranged in an order that can be related to children's changing needs as their experience of outdoor investigation increases.

Volume 1 is concerned with the earliest exploration beyond the classroom when children need experience that can sharpen their sensory perception and help them to think about the numerical and spatial aspects of their surroundings.

Usually this would apply to infants but older children, coming to field studies for the first time, will need some practice in early stages of the work before they become ready to deal with studies appropriate for more experienced investigators.

Volume 2 contains many questions and suggestions designed to help children work actively and purposefully on studies in depth. They become ready to do this when they find something of particular interest on which they wish to focus attention.

Volume 3 could serve as an impetus to children's investigation of some major biological ideas and relationships through the design of controlled experiments. They should be able to deal with the reasoning this involves as their capacity for abstract thought develops.

Volume 4 is relevant to fieldwork at all times. It deals with ways and means of providing the facilities, equipment and raw materials children need for all stages of their outdoor investigations and resulting activities on their return to study areas in school.

A book concerned with the countryside should create awareness of the many ways in which living things and environmental conditions affect each other, so suggestions for studying these relationships and the consequences of disturbing them have been included. Every future citizen requires this knowledge as a basis for responsible attitudes towards the use of land and natural resources (ie *conservation*) in view of the ever-increasing demands a rising world population and desire for better standards of living will continue to make on the world's finite stores of materials.

Although this book is about children it is not for them; it is a book for teachers and it could not have been written without their help. Many teachers, and in particular some in Derbyshire and Kent, have contributed directly or indirectly to its contents. They have done so by encouraging children to pursue scientific interests, share common experiences and record what seems significant to them. They have collected questions children have asked, described models they have designed and noted suggestions and problems that have absorbed their attention. In this way a large collection of ideas has emerged from children's purposeful activity, guided carefully by thoughtful teachers. This is now available as a source of inspiration from which other teachers can select when children they know, show by their questions and behaviour, that they are near the end of their own ideas and resources and need contact with the greater experience of an interested adult.

Children experimenting with the growth of sycamore seedlings

1 Children tackling problems

Continuing intellectual development; experience of different places and things

What can we expect when these influences are at work on children moving through the middle years of school life (nine to thirteen years of age) ? We can soon find out if we join the children at work.

Growing self-heal

This time we will begin in a small rural school in Derbyshire where all the children between nine and eleven years of age form a teaching group. One summer these children spent a considerable amount of time trying to produce their own collections of common wild flowers by growing them from seeds. Their first attempts in pots and trays in the classroom came to grief through erratic watering, but when they were given fresh supplies of seeds and their teacher put a piece of the garden attached to her school house at their disposal they set about the job with renewed determination.

One group concentrated on self-heal (*Prunella vulgaris*) and cultivated it in a sheltered sunny corner. They kept their plants generously supplied with manure and water and regularly removed all weeds from their surroundings. They were delighted with the large succulent plants they soon produced. Small stunted specimens of the same plant were very common on the dry limestone grassland around the village. In fact they produced the seeds the children used. One day while I was at the school talking with the children and their teacher about this work a nine-year-old girl tugged at my sleeve and said, 'If you change what you give them they grow differently, don't they ?'

Here was something very different from the collecting and the sensory observation and sorting of infant and younger junior children. This nine-year-old had referred back in

her mind to her recent experience of caring for the self-heal plants in the garden and compared these results with the wild specimens on the hillside that received no human attention and the previous set of plants which had died. She was suggesting a reason for the differences she found interesting. It was time to encourage this child to test her ideas by growing plants under different environmental conditions.

Planting seeds

In another small school, a few miles away, the same task of growing wild flowers from seeds was also tackled, but with different results as we can see from this extract of a letter from the headmaster.

'Originally my class planted forty-two seeds but only produced two plants. The children in Mrs Parson's class grew eighteen plants from sixty-two seeds while the infants had the misfortune to have all their seeds scratched up by hens.

Of seeds that were taken home, two lots were dug up deliberately by angry fathers who thought they had sufficient weeds without cultivating more, and two other settings were accidentally dug up. One girl managed to grow four red campions after her dog had scratched among the newly planted seeds.

Although we do not seem to have been very successful, honestly believe that the children have learned a great deal about seed planting. Now that they realise we have failed to produce many plants they are beginning to seek out the reasons.'

The matter could not be allowed to rest there, since the children were ready to be interested in the reasons for their results. When I next visited that school I told the junior class something about the way Charles Darwin worked in his garden at Downe and read them the following extract from Ruth Moore's biography.*

'One spring he [Darwin] measured off in his own garden a 2 ft by 3 ft piece of ground and had it dug up and cleared. Every day on his walks he stopped to mark each seedling that came up. By the end of the season 357 seedlings had pushed their heads above the ground. There was no choking by other plants in this little plot but 295 of them were destroyed, principally by slugs and insects. The weeds' struggle for existence was a severe one, 83 per cent perished.

'Darwin also sowed fifteen kinds of seeds in his meadow where there was competition from other plants already established, fifteen of the seeds germinated but died rapidly—not one succeeded in flowering.'

These children, like Darwin, became interested in the struggle for survival continually going on between living things. They wanted to find the answers to questions such as

How many seeds can one plant produce?
What would happen if all seeds became plants?
What prevents this?

Moore, R., Charles Darwin *(Hutchinson, 1957).*

Finding problems to tackle

There is no doubt that some children in the upper classes of junior and middle schools are ready to do more than collect information about their surroundings. As their skill in comparing their experiences and observations grows, more unsuspected differences and similarities will come to their notice, causing them to think 'That's strange ....' Then as they grow older they ask themselves more frequently 'I wonder why ...' and in this way they find problems to tackle.

These children need teachers who can recognise and respond to their growing interest in reasons for things that seem curious.

An investigation using snails

Three eleven-year-old girls studying snails found in the school grounds during June and July had a teacher of the right sort. As they worked they consulted various reference books. They read that snails hibernate in winter after forming a structure called an epiphragm across the mouth of the shell for protection.

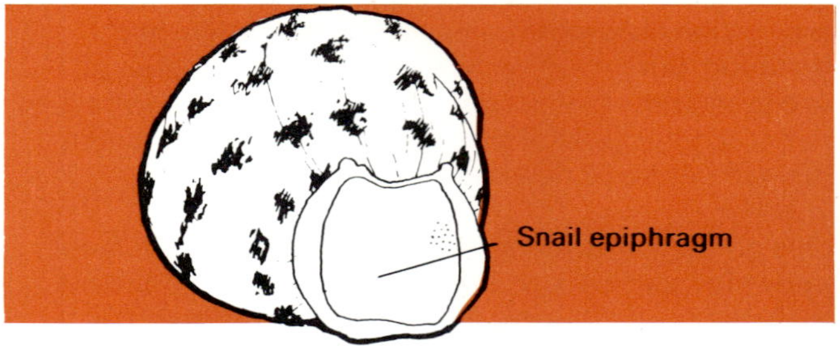

They asked their teacher whether it would be possible to get their snails to form epiphragms by making them colder. In this situation a teacher might well be tempted to tell children that the easiest way to get snails to produce a thinner variety of this membrane in summer is to keep them in dry conditions for a short time in a box, but he was wiser. He challenged the girls to think of a way of testing their suggestion.

They collected a number of garden snails (*Helix aspersa*), put similar supplies of food in six identical large Kilner jars, placed equal numbers of snails in each jar, packed ice obtained from the canteen refrigerator round three jars and left the others at room temperature. They maintained the temperature difference between these jars for the next two weeks, renewing the ice regularly. No epiphragms were formed but the snails in the colder jars became more sluggish and ate less. Possibly this was the first stage in the slowing down of metabolism characteristic of hibernation.

Snails in cold conditions and at room temperature

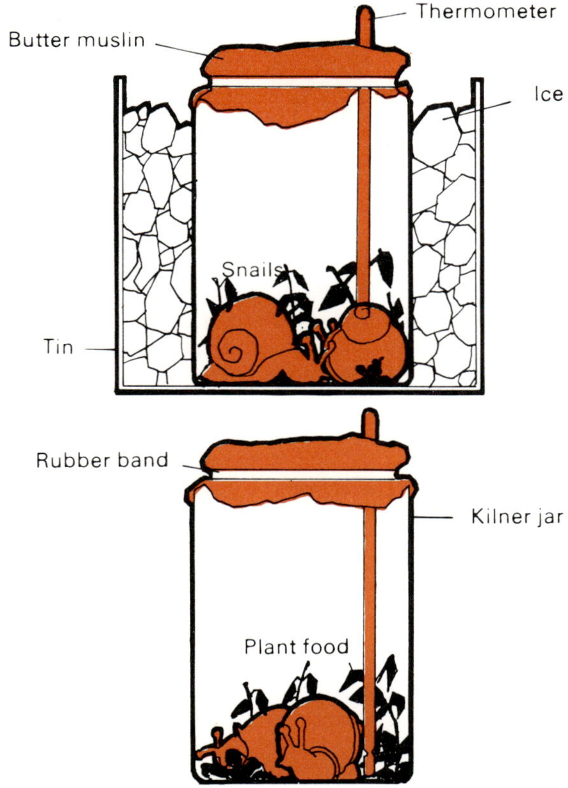

This is a case where the testing of an idea failed to yield a definite result. The teacher, who had rightly held back earlier, now came into the picture for more helpful consultation.

Perhaps the snails should be given more time.
A book might give more information about their habits; this could be checked.
Snails are more easily found in wet weather. Would it be a good idea to try the effect of dry conditions?

It would certainly have been quicker and less trouble for the teacher to have told the girls what to do as soon as they became curious. But the time they spent in trying to find out information, rather than taking short cuts to it, was well spent, if judged by the quality of the girls' thinking, their increasing curiosity about the animals' behaviour and their desire to continue investigating.

Scientific method

While this example of the girls' experiment is fresh in the mind it is appropriate to draw attention to the difference between experience and experimentation, for this is something many dealing with the scientific interests of young children often find confusing.

When six-year-old Michael (described in Volume 1, pages 78–79) looked carefully at the sands and soils in his collection, rubbed small quantities of them between his fingers and listened while shaking jars partly filled with these materials, he was doing all he could think of to find out what his specimens were like. Through these *experiences* he gained knowledge of some of their properties.

The thought processes of the girls with the snails were much more logical and complex. They drew on their own memories of what they had read to suggest a possible way of inducing their own specimens to produce protective epiphragms. They then deliberately imagined a course of action through which their suggestion could be tested and, since this seemed a sensible way of going about things, tried it out. Such a test of a hypothesis, for that is the scientific name given to a suggested explanation or answer to a question, is a genuine scientific experiment.

The experimenters can use the results of their investigation as evidence to support or disprove their original idea.

Gaining knowledge and understanding of the universe through the testing of hypothetical suggestions, or, as we often say, by scientific method, has been one of man's greatest intellectual and creative achievements.

The value of helping all future citizens to appreciate this is one of the strongest reasons for including scientific studies in their education.

An investigation using plantains

It is not always necessary to test hypotheses by experiments. On many occasions children will be able to gather support for, or evidence against, their ideas by making further observations.

Some twelve-year-old children found considerable differences in the size of the leaves of broad-leaved plantain plants (*Plantago major*) growing in the lanes around a day field centre from which they were working.

The reasons they were soon able to offer for some plantain plants having larger leaves were: shady conditions; the presence of other tall plants around them.

It should be possible to check these suggestions by measuring more plantain leaves. They were guided in planning a more systematic investigation by their teacher's questions.

From where shall we collect some more sets of plantain leaves?

(Sunny places where most plants are tall.)
(Sunny places where most plants are short.)
(Shady places where most plants are tall.)
(Shady places where most plants are short.)

How many leaves should be collected from each place? (24–30.)

How can we obtain leaves from plants at similar stages of growth? (Look for plants with flowering spikes at the same stage.)

What shall we measure on each leaf? (The greatest length and width.)

What shall we do with each set of measurements to make comparisons easier? (Find their average or mean.)

The children's measurements supported their suggestion that plantains with the larger leaves were those among other tall plants. This was the case in both shady and sunny places. Sets of leaves from plantains not competing with tall plants were decidedly smaller but the average dimensions of those from shady places a little larger than those exposed to more sunshine.

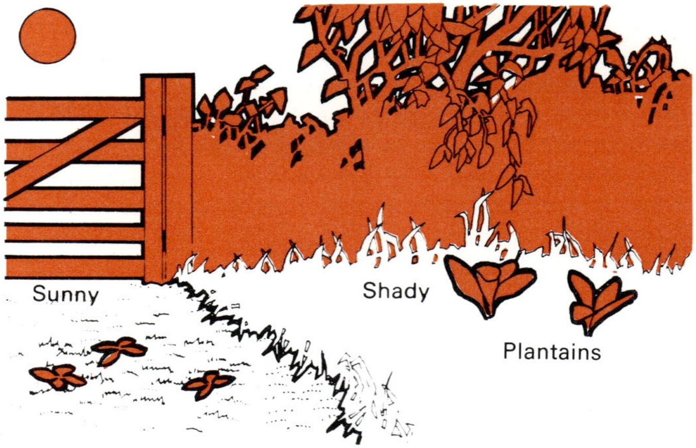

These results soon gave rise to further questions.

Is large leaf size in plantains influenced by both shading and the presence of other tall plants?
Is one of these conditions more important than the other?
To what extent do other tall plants shade plantains in sunny places?
Do these conditions affect the leaf size of other plants?
Can we find any other conditions that seem to go with small leaves?
What about treading on plants? Plants on pathways seem to be small.

We have not tried to compare the leaves of plantains growing in dry and damp places.

The further children try to take this kind of work the greater their chances of understanding the continuing nature of scientific investigation.

A number of environmental conditions are likely to influence the development of an interesting feature. The results of their course of observations and experiments may convince children that certain of their suggestions are on the right track. Yet the possibility always remains that some further testing, carried out in a different way, may provide evidence against this. A hypothetical idea can be disproved, it can be reinforced and supported by evidence, but never finally proved. On many occasions willingness to take new evidence into account has brought about advances in scientific knowledge of great benefit to mankind.

Hypothetical thinking

It is obvious that children will not be capable of suggesting hypotheses and testing them by imaginative experiments and observations until their intellectual development is sufficiently advanced to enable them to relate in their minds experience gained at different times. Work bearing on science for children who have not developed this capacity for abstract thought should consist of investigation, comparison and sorting of things they find in different surroundings. In this way they can accumulate a pool of remembered experience from which, at a later stage, they can draw the ideas they need for making hypothetical suggestions and devising ways of testing them.

The ability to think hypothetically about problems and to imagine courses of action comes at different times.

Befriending a fox

A certain gifted child was just seven when she produced a book describing how her family befriended an injured fox for a fortnight and then let it go. Her memories caused her to suspect that this same animal was returning to her garden at night to drink milk put out for a local hedgehog. This is what she wrote about the observations she made to check this idea.

'So the night after that night we decided to stop up and see who it was of course we had to plead to my mum because normally we go to bed at seven o'clock but tonight we went at eight o'clock because the thing that was drinking the milk came just before it was eight o'clock—now we were indoors and we heard a Squeak and we rushed to the window and to our great surprise it was the fox it still had the bandage on thats how we new it was the same fox because mummy left the bandage my daddy went out and got it and my mummy took the bandage off and from that night onwards we have always put milk out and when we look the next morning its allways gone and last of all we allways hear a squeaking noise.'

Ability at such an early age to refer to the suspected fox as 'the thing' when unsure of its identity and support the statements which followed with evidence is very rare. However, even this child did not think in such a logical way all the time. A few days after she had completed her account, her teacher placed the skull and lower jaw bones of a fox on the nature table, but her next piece of writing simply showed that she and her friend enjoyed pretending that these specimens were their own false teeth when their teacher was not looking.

It is obvious that nothing will be gained by forcing the pace. Teachers must expect to deal with some children between nine and thirteen years who are still at the stage of gathering experience and others who are able to reason logically, who should therefore be encouraged to speculate about the causes of phenomena and to think of ways of testing their ideas.

Designing experiments

Even the most able children will need a good deal of assistance, through discussion with their teachers, when they begin trying to design experiments. This will often involve understanding the use of a *control* and the necessity of dealing with *variables*.

Continuing the work with snails

The girls who tried to check whether cooling caused snails to form epiphragms found that it was not enough just to make a jar of these animals as cold as possible. It was easier to judge whether colder conditions were having any effect when the snails exposed to low temperatures could be compared with similar sets at normal room temperature.

Things undergoing treatment nearest to normal conditions (middle of the range) serve as controls against which other things exposed to extremes can be measured.

In this same experiment the girls were very careful to make sure that conditions other than temperature that might influence the creature's behaviour, such as their size, the amount and type of their food supplies and space in the jars for movement, were similar in all trials. By doing this they greatly increased the possibility of any differences between the sets of snails being due to the temperature differences they had deliberately created.

In any experimental situation it is necessary to consider all the conditions that can be altered (the variables). After deciding on the one that is to be varied, there must also be arrangements for other conditions likely to influence results to be kept as similar as possible in all trials. Conditions unlikely to affect the outcome of the tests can be ignored.

The need to make allowances for individual differences in the same types of plants or animals by using large numbers of them, or by repeating tests in the same way and averaging results, must also be borne in mind.

Results that do not agree with expectations can be most useful in developing skill in experimental design. The snails that did not form epiphragms provided the girls with good reasons for reconsidering the situation, trying out different ideas, and so adding to their knowledge of the animals' habits.

On the other hand, it is equally important that teachers should not undermine children's confidence when they make use of their own ideas by too much emphasis, too soon, on accuracy and validity. Early attempts to design experiments and the apparatus involved will be poor, if judged by adult standards. Only the experience of experimenting, aided by constant discussion with teachers, will enable children to become more adept at spotting possible causes of error and so see for themselves how to improve on their first attempts. When children cannot decide how to take an investigation all the way and their interest in the problem seems to be evaporating it may be better for their teachers to be satisfied with incomplete attempts. If children are not discouraged, they can always bring more experience to bear on a similar problem at a later stage and then do more with it.

Interest in solving problems

Although the countryside can be a never-failing source of good investigations, there are children who fail to discover how interesting and exciting the work of solving problems can be. This often happens when they have been made to use techniques for estimating the numbers of plants and animals in different places before they have found good reasons for wanting such information. Children need to find their problems first through general observation, making comparisons and asking questions about interesting differences and similarities thus brought to light.

The blackbird's nest

When children discover problems they really wish to solve they will carry out monotonous or difficult tasks with great persistence. Two eleven-year-old girls studying the habits of birds coming to their school grounds found a deserted blackbird's nest. They took this to pieces and discovered that thick and thin twigs, straw, dog hairs, wool, wood shavings, grass and moss had been used in its construction. Then from the point of discovery of the nest, they searched for the nearest source of supply of each material and they measured the distances between these and the place where the nest was found. They found the shortest distance the blackbird would have to fly to collect in turn one piece of each material used.
Then by dividing each material into amounts that a blackbird could carry in its beak they were able to make a rough calculation of the shortest distance that must have been flown in collecting all the materials for the nest. Their records showed that they were well aware that much greater distances might have been involved if the bird went further afield for its material. In accumulating this evidence of blackbirds' industry when engaged in building a nest they stuck to their task with unflagging zeal. Having done this they went on to work out a way of comparing the number of wing beats different birds made between two landmarks as they flew over the school grounds.

Objectives

The value of discussion in helping children to discover and tackle scientific problems is obvious, but the teachers should be clear in their own minds about the type of experiences likely to be significant and the ways in which children should be encouraged to think about them.

Here is a summary that may help teachers to formulate their own objectives for this consultative role.

Experience and thought leading to the discovery of problems

1. Exploring places in search of interesting things to observe and compare.

2. Collecting quantitative evidence of differences and similarities.

3. Becoming curious about reasons for whatever has been discovered (shown by more 'Why . . .' questions).

Experience and thought involved in tackling problems

1. Offering possible explanations for observations and situations that seem curious (that is, suggesting hypotheses).

2. Designing experiments or systematic observations to test such hypothetical ideas.

This will involve :

a. Thinking of possible courses of action and imagining their outcome (that is, making predictions).

b. Making decisions regarding :

The treatment to be varied on different sets of specimens.
Variables to be kept constant.

The use of a control.
The number of trials to be undertaken.
The number of specimens to be used for each trial.

c. Considering whether the proposed tests are fair.

3. Collecting or designing and constructing any apparatus required.

4. Carrying out experiments or observations as planned.

5. Observing results carefully and deciding whether these support or disprove the original hypothesis. (This may lead to much argument.)

6. Either making statements supported by evidence about findings, or asking further questions.

7. Realising that further investigations may throw new light on the problem and make a change of opinion necessary.

What should the children learn?

Teachers often ask whether there is any body of knowledge about the environment that they should help children to gain by the time they are thirteen years of age.

Since outdoor investigations and the work in schools to which they give rise should be concerned with the things children can find interesting in the places they visit, the sequence and emphasis of their work must vary, and a common programme with the objective of acquiring a common body of knowledge would be neither possible nor desirable. Yet we know that similar discoveries can often result from different experience, because of the underlying order and pattern that exist in the natural world. Here are some statements that generally apply to living things.

1. Plants and animals often affect each other, that is, they are interdependent.

2. Their numbers would increase rapidly if there were no checks.

3. The different parts of their bodies are well designed for the work they do, or we could say that there are many relationships between form and function.

4. Living things vary.

5. They are usually well adapted to their environment.

6. Their uneven distribution can often be related to differences in environmental conditions.

Although these general observations are important, and in fact, they were taken into account by Charles Darwin when he formulated his theory of evolution, it must be emphasised that teachers should not attempt to make them part of children's store of knowledge through theoretical teaching on particular occasions. Instead children need first-hand experience of plants and animals in relation to the surrounding environment and thus can gradually come to see for themselves that these statements hold good in most situations.

This book is concerned with such experience. While suggestions for studies have been grouped according to the ideas they illustrate, the investigations that children undertake should arise from the situations they encounter while exploring and the leading questions of their teachers.

2 The interdependence of living things

How many seeds has our sunflower produced?

The capacity to multiply

If all the plants and animals developed into adults, there would soon be overcrowding and severe competition. Does this happen ? How could the problems be solved ?

How many seeds?

Children's interest in the number of seeds single flowers produce makes a good class project.

In July they will be able to find many plants with some of their fruits formed, and some with their flowers still remaining. There will thus be plenty of material from which individual workers or pairs can choose plants to investigate. In discussing plans for developing this work teachers can help children to select plants with the larger fruits and seeds and so avoid difficulties.

With the help of their stereomicroscope children can discover which of their plants produce one-seeded fruits and which many-seeded, and the number of seeds these latter contain.

Our collection of fruits	
There was only one seed in the fruits on these plants	**Fruits on these plants contained many seeds**
Buttercup	Vetch
Dandelion	Foxglove
Goat's beard	Pea
Plantain	Shepherd's purse
Wheat	Poppy
Sunflower	Red campion
	Blackberry

Which plant is the biggest producer of seed ?

Counting the number of one-seeded fruits on a plant will also give the number of seeds.

How can the number of seeds from one generation of a plant be estimated when each fruit contains many seeds ?

When the children are comparing the results of their counts and estimations, they may make some critical observations. Here are some.

'All specimens of this plant may not produce the same number of seeds. Would it be better to find the average seed production of ten of these plants ?'

'If specimens of the same plants are grown under different conditions, may the number of seeds produced vary ?'

This suggestion is worth testing.

1. Soak some peas from the same packet. Then sow them all in the same part of the school garden. Place half of them very close together and half spaced according to the directions on the packet. Compare the number of seeds produced by each set.

Could any other factor, besides spacing, be having some influence on the seed production ?

2. If you can find some bluebell plants in the same part of a wood, some of which are under trees and others fully exposed to sunlight in a clearing, compare after flowering the seed production of ten of the plants similar in size from each place.

Some children may be interested in making more ambitious estimations of fruit and seed production.

1. A horse chestnut tree in full bloom.

How many conkers (the seeds of the horse chestnut) might come from this tree in autumn ?
What is the average number of flowers in each cluster ?
About how many clusters of flowers can be seen when facing the tree ?
Would it be fair to assume that there are a similar number of clusters of flowers on the other side of the tree ?

When the flowering stage is over we could try to discover how many flowers in a cluster usually form fruits.
Some fruits may contain more than one conker.

Would it be easier to estimate the number of clusters of flowers by counting those seen through a frame on different parts of the tree and totalling results ?

Dotted lines indicate parts seen through frame

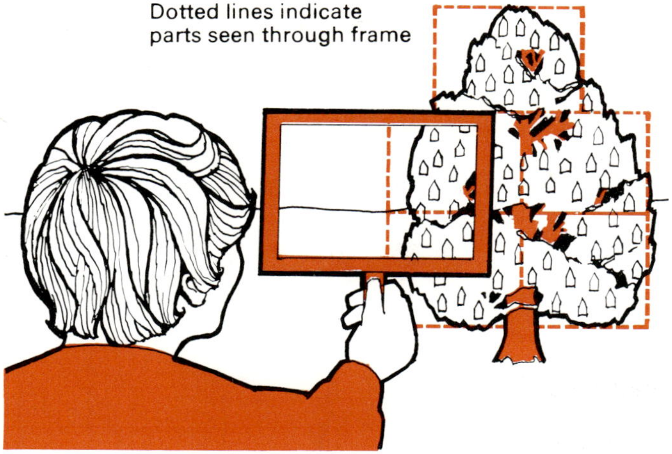

2. Poppies in a cornfield.

Sometimes in a badly cultivated cornfield many poppies can be found fairly evenly distributed.

What is the average number of seeds one poppy head is likely to produce? Many children can share the labour of discovering this.
How many poppy plants in a square metre?
How many square metres are infested with these weeds?
What can the farmer do to avoid the trouble that could be caused by all these poppies shedding their seeds?

A similar type of investigation could be carried out on a conspicuous patch of poppies growing on a roadside verge.

How many new animals?

1. How many eggs in:

A length of pond snail spawn?
A mass of frog spawn?
A ribbon of toad spawn?
A patch laid by a butterfly?

Mating toads

Take averages of ten counts if possible.

2 Collect some masses of empty egg cases of the common whelk (*Buccinium undatum*) from the seashore.

What is the average number of eggs these masses probably contained at one time?
Were all the collections of cases similiar in size?

3. How many eggs does a cubic centimetre of the hard roe of a female herring contain? What is the volume of all this roe?

The female cod is capable of laying a very large number of eggs. Look out for pieces of this roe in a fishmonger's shop. One roe represents one ovary. One roe was found to measure about 20 × 9 × 4 cm. What volume is this?
Try to discover the number of eggs in a cubic centimetre of a female cod's roe, then try to estimate the number of eggs the roe described above might contain. Does a cubic centimetre of cod roe appear to contain more or less eggs than the same volume of herring roe?

4. In May it is easy to find masses of aphids on the young shoots of sycamore trees. Some children could try to find out more about the rate at which these insects increase.

Place two aphids in the container, as shown, with the normal food supply. Count the number of aphids in the cage on the same day of each week. Plot the results of the count on squared paper.

Insect cage

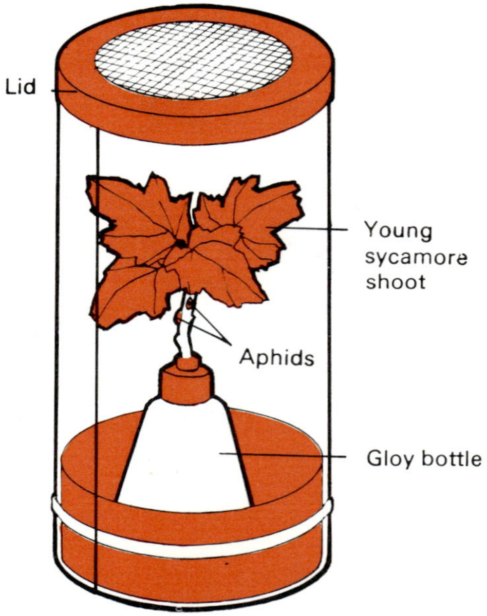

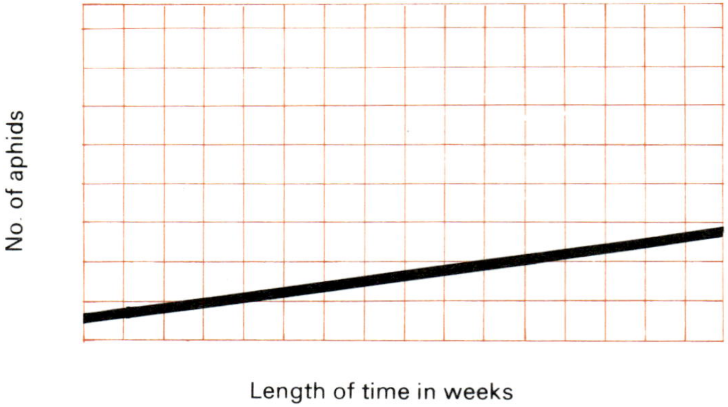

5. If locusts are kept in the school, some of the females can be isolated after copulation and their eggs counted.

6. Use an observation beehive to observe and count the egg-laying activities of the queen bee.

Speculation about the rate of increase

The above investigations have been concerned with one generation of individuals only. Children will probably enjoy dealing with some mathematical calculations illustrating the possible results of the unchecked increase of certain plants and animals.

1. How much ground space does a full-grown specimen of the plant you are studying occupy in its normal habitat?

If five generations of seeds produced by this plant all germinate and develop successfully how much space will they require, assuming that the number of seeds produced is similar on each occasion?

2. How many common pond snails (*Limnaea stagnalis*) can we keep in our classroom aquarium for scavenging without making too heavy a demand on the food supplies in it?

How many aquariums would you need to accommodate in good living conditions all the pond snails that could develop from one length of spawn laid by each of these creatures?

Some children may like to draw upon their findings in order to set their classmates similar problems.

In the course of discussion the children's attention could also be drawn to the fact that the reproduction rate of some plants and animals is still not enough to meet man's demands for food. They might discuss, for example, over-fishing and the cod war; and over-harvesting.

Checks to survival

When children in their investigations and calculations discover the problems that could be created by the survival of all the seeds, eggs and offspring produced by living things, they will probably begin to speculate on ways in which this may be checked. Much interesting work can develop from attempts to test such speculations.

Do all seeds produced by plants germinate?

Collect complete generations of seeds produced by suitable single plants, such as wheat, pea, vetch, burdock, cleavers, sunflower. Use these for germination trials.

If children discover that some seeds fail to continue their growth, it is easier for them to realise that this may happen to animals too. Do all the eggs in a poultry farmer's incubators hatch successfully? Even when wild birds' eggs hatch, many young fall from the nest in spring and perish.

Does chance play a part in the failure of some seeds to become plants?

This could be a class investigation. Make three collections of sycamore fruits from the ground during July and August:

Those found in conditions favourable to germination.
Those found in unfavourable conditions.
Those shed at too early a stage for development to continue.

What percentage does each of these groups form of the total number collected?
Make further searches for sycamore fruits in places unfavourable to germination. Are there any conditions in these places that may help some of the fruits to be moved again?

Note that there is also a good chance that eggs scattered in large numbers by many creatures, such as cod, herring, sea urchins, may be eaten or damaged before they hatch.

Make a list of creatures that do take care of their eggs and/or young. Do these animals lay many eggs or have many young ones?

Competition between plants

When plants and animals are competing for essential needs like food, space and light, some will be successful and flourish. Do the losers perish ?

A study of sycamore seedlings

These seedlings repay investigation because it is fairly easy to estimate their ages. When buds giving rise to new shoots open, their scale leaves fall, leaving rings known as girdle scars surrounding the twig. The part of a twig between two sets of girdle scars represents a year's growth.

Sycamore seedlings in first, second and third year of growth

Make a search in woodland or on a piece of waste ground near sycamore trees for areas containing many sycamore seedlings.

Examine all of them for girdle scars. Calculate the percentages in the first, second and third or more years of age.

Does an examination of sycamore seedlings in similar areas give similar results ? Assuming the supply of seeds to such areas to be approximately the same each year, does the study provide any evidence of a struggle to survive ? If so, at what age are most seedlings eliminated ?

Do some plants make conditions unfavourable for others ?

Find a piece of ground that is completely covered by one conspicuous plant such as thistles, stinging nettles, bracken. Clear all specimens of this plant from a patch about 2 m square. Make sure all the underground stems of these plants are removed.

Then keep a record with dates of any plants that become established on this plot. Do some species appear that did not obtain growing space before ?

If children can keep this investigation going indefinitely, they can discover whether the new immigrant plants maintain their hold or whether the original plants again take over the land.

Long-term investigations of bare patches of ground or seed boxes and old sinks filled with soil will often show that some plants are more aggressive than others, and by their rapid spread will drive out plants that may have appeared and become established earlier.

A study of weeds

These are the successful aggressors, plants that man continually tries to remove from the ground he cultivates. Yet they appear season after season and soon take over neglected land. What makes them do so well ?

Ask children each to collect the six most common weeds they can discover in flower beds, borders, allotments or cultivated fields. Use this material as a basis for observation and discussion. The children can suggest reasons why these plants appear and spread successfully, and their ideas can be recorded on a class chart.

Here is an example of the type of work that might emerge.

Why is it difficult to get rid of weeds?

No.	Weed characteristics: children's suggestions	Possible advantages to plant	Examples
1	Can grow very close to ground with leaves forming rosette.	Not removed by lawn mower. All leaves receive plenty of light.	Dandelion, daisy, broad-leaved plantain.
2	Weak stem due to rapid growth. Has means of attaching itself to other plants for support.	Leaves receive plenty of light.	Bindweed, cleavers, white and black bryony, ivy.
3	Long main root.	Difficult to remove by digging.	Dandelion, sheep's parsley, hogweed, field bindweed.
4	Produces much pollen widely scattered by wind.	Many plants likely to be pollinated.	Grasses, sycamore flowers.
5	Flowers widely open.	Can be pollinated by many types of insect.	Buttercup, rock rose.
6	Many seeds produced.	Good chance of some seeds finding suitable growing conditions.	Willow-herb, poppy, groundsel, dandelion, sow-thistle, fleabane, field-thistle, sheep's parsley.
7	Short life cycle, with two or more generations in a season.	Many seeds produced so greater chance of some finding suitable places for germination.	Groundsel, shepherd's purse, red dead nettle.
8	Good aids to fruit and seed dispersal.	Greater chance of seeds finding suitable conditions for germination. Reduces overcrowding.	Dandelion, groundsel, goat's beard, field-thistle, sow-thistle, cleavers, willow-herb.
9	Can increase by parts of itself growing.	Can spread very rapidly.	Creeping buttercup, couch-grass, dandelion, mouse-ear hawkweed, stinging nettle.
10	Has protective devices such as spines, stings, etc.	Not removed by grazing animals.	Stinging nettle, thistle.
11	Inconspicuous flowers.	Not collected by people.	Mugwort, fat hen, spurge, ground-elder.
12	Hardy, so does not die quickly in difficult conditions.	Survival enables further increase.	Couch-grass, dandelion, stinging nettle, plantain.

Much interesting practical work can follow. Groups of children can try to discover whether their suggestions on the chart apply to other weeds they find nearby.

In the following suggestions for further work, the numbers are keyed to the numbers in the chart.

1. Weeds in rosette form.

Examine a regularly mown lawn. Make a list of any plants you find there apart from grass. Which occur most frequently? How many have green leaves arranged in the form of a rosette in close contact with the ground? Can you find any of the same type of plant growing among taller plants? How are the leaves arranged then? Are any of their surfaces in close contact with the ground?

Mark out a square metre on the lawn containing some dandelions. Leave the grass in this plot unmown. Do the leaves of the dandelions remain very close to the ground?

2. Weeds whose stems grow rapidly.

Make a list of all the plants climbing in a 50-m length of hedgerow. Try to find the methods by which they attach themselves to more sturdy plants. Measure the longest internodes you can find on ten specimens of a climbing plant such as one of the following: cleavers, hedge bindweed (convolvulus), white bryony, black bryony, ivy.

How does the average of these ten measurements compare with the average length of the longest internodes on ten hawthorn or privet twigs?

A similar comparison can be made between the stems of field bindweed (climber) and the herbaceous plants they twine round.

Cut 15-cm lengths of stems of cleavers, convolvulus, hawthorn and privet. Choose pieces of the same thickness. Try to attach them in vertical positions to lumps of Plasticine. Which pieces of stem remain upright?

Find the average heights of ten small specimens of cleavers and ten small specimens of a hedgerow plant using no support such as jack-in-the-hedge or hedge woundwort. Continue measuring the heights of all of these plants on alternate days and calculate the average increase of both sets.

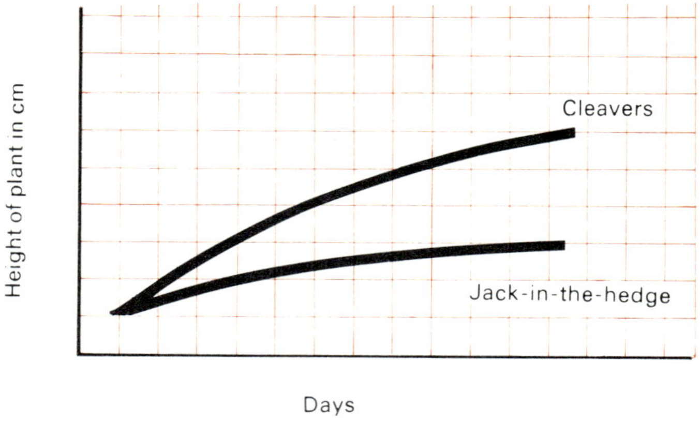

3. Weeds with long main roots.

A class competition can be held for finding the weed with the longest root.

4. Weeds that produce much pollen.

During May and June find out the daily pollen count by looking in the *Daily Telegraph* under 'Weather'. Do high counts coincide with any particular weather conditions? Which plants at this time of year appear to be producing much pollen? Put some in a jar standing on a sheet of black paper. Is much pollen shed?

5. Weeds with widely open flowers.

The insect visitors to flowers in a border, some with wide openings into their corollas and some with small ones, can be recorded by pairs of children for a given period of time such as 15 or 30 minutes (see chart at top of next page).

Flowers	Flies	Beetles	Bumble bees	Honey bees	Wasps	Ants
Meadow buttercup	𝍸	III		I	I	IIII
Vetch				IIII		
Clover				𝍸 III		
Hogweed	𝍸	IIII			III	II
White dead nettle			III	IIII		
Rock rose	IIII	IIII			I	II

Calm sunny days are best for this investigation as then insects are more active. Which plants had the greatest variety of visitors ?

6. Weeds producing many seeds.

Try to estimate the number of seeds produced by each of three of the commonest weeds in the school grounds (see page 12).

7. Weeds with short life-cycles.

Collect some seeds of shepherd's purse and dandelion and sow them in seed trays. Keep them well watered. When the seeds from these plants are ripe, collect them and plant them. Continue this work by trying to discover the number of generations that can be produced in six months.

How soon do seedlings of these plants appear after planting ?

8. Weeds with good aids to fruit and seed dispersal.

What aids to dispersal can you find on the fruits of the following weeds : dandelion, willow-herb, thistle, cleavers ? See also suggestions on pages 52–56.

9. Weeds that increase when parts of themselves grow.

Collect some roots of dandelion or field bindweed plants. Cut them into pieces of the following lengths : 0·5, 1·0, 1·5, 2·0, 2·5, 3·0, 3·5, 4·0 cm, etc.
Plant the pieces ten to a box in seed boxes containing John Innes compost. Record the number of plants produced. The roots of these plants produce adventitious stem buds, so very small portions are able to grow.

For a long-term study, find a specimen of a young weed that produces runners, such as creeping buttercup, mouse-ear hawkweed, wild strawberry, or one that produces rhizomes, such as yarrow, stinging nettle, couch grass. Clear the ground around the specimen. As time passes, observe the number of new plants that develop from the original plant.

10. Weeds having protective devices.

Sometimes patches of stinging nettles appear in parts of a field where cow pats have fallen. If cows are grazing in such a field, do they make any attempt to feed on the stinging nettles ? How much can be discovered with the aid of a good stereomicroscope about the stinging device of stinging nettles ? Can any evidence of animals feeding on thistles be found ? If so, are these small insects or large domestic animals ? Is the whole plant eaten or, only part of its leaves ?

11. Weeds with inconspicuous flowers.

What are the favourite wild flowers of all the children

between eleven and thirteen years of age in the school? How could such a survey be made efficiently? Is there any relationship between the preferences expressed and large and brightly coloured flowers?

Which very common local flowers were not mentioned by any children? Can any reasons for this be suggested?

12. Hardy weeds.

Make collections of plants found flourishing in the following places:

Heavily trampled ground near the entrance to a field where cattle graze.
Between cracks in the pavements of city streets.
Beneath a thick hedge in very dim light.
In the sour soil of a very neglected urban front garden.

What common weeds in the neighbourhood are perennials? How do they survive during the coldest months of the year?

Conservation

Conservationists become concerned about the rapid spread of aggressive plants at the expense of rare or more interesting species. Some boys from a secondary school in Kent carried out some interesting work in this field on a nature reserve established by the Kent Trust for Nature Conservation at Hunsted Woods near Canterbury.

These woods contain a natural sphagnum bog which is continually threatened by the invasion of birch seedlings which create unfavourable conditions for the moss by removing much water from the soil.

The boys tried to raise the water-table in the bog by constructing a dam across a small stream running into it. They also removed many birch seedlings from some parts of the bog and then tried to compare the growth of sphagnum there with that in areas of similar size where birch seedlings were left.

Attempting to raise the water table

The nature reserve at Hothfield Common near Ashford (Kent), contains another interesting sphagnum bog. Members of the Ecology Group of the Kent Field Club removed birch seedlings from part of it and then made a comparative study of the plant life there and also in another part of the bog where no conservation work was attempted. Their efforts did not lead to the sphagnum moss increasing in the first area. Instead, some plants not previously recorded in the marshy area became established. Removing the birch seedlings evidently made conditions more favourable for them. This shows that the task of conservation can be far from straightforward. So many things can happen when environmental conditions are altered.

Bracken, a plant that harbours few species of animals, will sometimes take over heathland previously dominated by heather. The spread of bracken can be controlled by breaking off its young shoots in May or early June and then again in autumn. It is said that this can be done quickly by dragging a heavy chain over the ground. This is an interesting idea that children might try testing if they can find some waste ground where bracken grows and where they wish to establish a greater variety of species.

Animals using plants

Animals' demands for food and sheltered breeding places may damage plants and so prevent or reduce their fruit and seed production. Here is an extreme example.

A field of maize devastated by locusts

Fortunately, this sort of devastation is not usual in this country; and it is being brought under control abroad by spraying. Farmers and gardeners can supply plenty of information about damage to their crops by other animal pests.

Damage to leaves

Carbohydrates are manufactured from raw materials in plant leaves. Interference with this process is likely to reduce the vitality of plants as these materials are a source of energy. An investigation of some of the things that damage leaves would therefore be worth tackling.

Here in chart form are some of the discoveries that might be made by children.

Our collection of damaged leaves		
Plants	**Animals responsible**	**Reason for attack**
Stinging nettle	Caterpillars of tortoiseshell butterfly	Food requirements
Cabbage Nasturtium	Caterpillars of cabbage white butterfly	Food requirements
Leaves in a herbaceous border	Slugs and snails	Food requirements
Sow-thistle Holly	Leaf-mining insects	Food and shelter for part of life history
Willow Oak	Gall-forming insects	Food and shelter for part of life history
Potomageton	China-mark moth	Food and shelter for part of life history

Make a collection of leaves showing signs of damage or unusual growths or marking.

Examine these specimens carefully to see whether they can be grouped according to the causes of the abnormalities, such as animals' need for food, shelter, etc.

How serious is the damage that animals do to plant leaves?

Leaf damaged by caterpillar

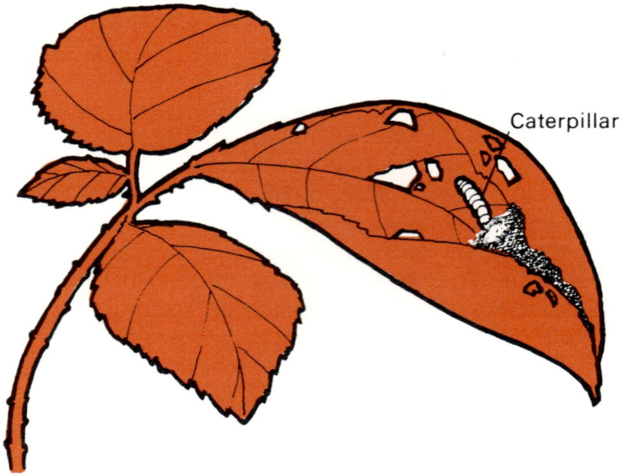

In the course of this work children are also likely to find many leaves damaged by fungi.

Leaf damaged by fungus

Take a sample of a hundred holly or sow-thistle leaves and find the number affected by the attacks of leaf-mining insects.

What is the length of the longest mine that can be found?

Approximately what area of the leaves remain for other purposes?

Is it possible to collect any evidence showing that plants with damaged leaves produce fewer flowers and seeds than undamaged plants?

This investigation can lead to some very worthwhile discussion about the balance in nature between feeders and food supplies. What happens if creatures destroy their own food supplies? The children could think about whether they ever do so.

Damage to fruits

Many creatures such as squirrels use acorns for food, and some woodland insects spend part of their life histories in the seeds.

Collect a sample of a hundred acorns.
Find out how many have been attacked by grubs.
Does this invasion affect the size of the acorns?

Make a grading device and use it to test the sizes of a sample of a hundred acorns collected from the ground beneath an oak tree.

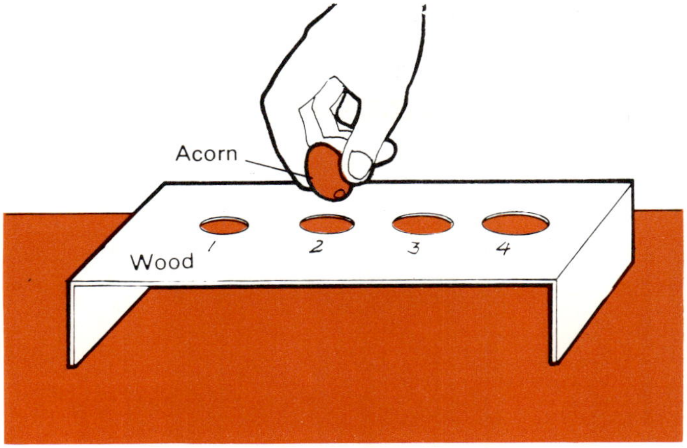

When the acorns have been sorted according to the holes they pass through, examine each set for damage by animals. Calculate the percentage affected in each case.

Can damaged acorns produce new plants? You can tell if acorns are damaged by looking for holes, marks, parts eaten away. Plant some in pots or the school garden. Keep them well watered and make a record of any growth that occurs.

Plants using animals

There are some plants that use animals. These are rare and so they should *not* be collected when they are discovered.

Try to capture a small insect with a pooter. Put it on one of the leaves of either a sundew or butterwort plant.

An insect trapped by sundew

If you should find bladderwort in a stream one or two of its bladders could be removed and examined with the aid of a stereomicroscope for small captive animals.

Do small insects that become trapped within cuckoo-pint flowers die?

What could you do to find out?

Competition between animals

The need for food causes rivalry, competition, gain and loss. Looking at birds will help children to understand something about this.

Bird watching

Scatter some food on a garden lawn. Winter and spring are the best times for this.

Which birds drive others away from it most vigorously ?

How do they do this ? By aggressive movements—sounds, pecking, etc.

Do they drive away birds like themselves or only different species ?

Do birds that have been driven off return to make further attempts to obtain food ?

Suspend a bag of shelled peanuts from a bird table. Which birds stake the strongest claim to this ? Which birds do they try to drive away ? Which garden birds do not compete for these nuts ?

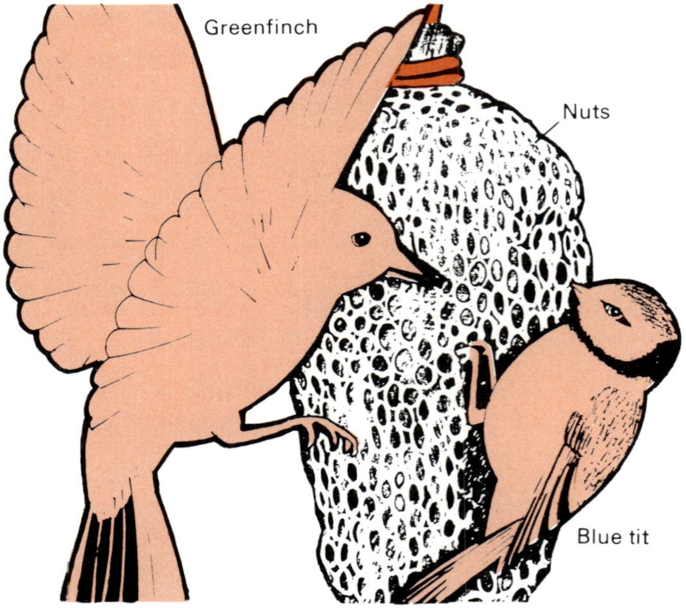

A male blackbird looking for food is a common sight in a garden. What happens if another male blackbird appears and tries to hunt in the same area ?

It is often interesting to look at the poultry when visiting a farm. Do any of the birds peck others and drive them away from food ? Which one seems to do this most successfully ? How near is an inferior bird allowed to approach, and does it behave in the same way towards any other bird ?

Is it possible to suggest a pecking order for these birds ? Does the farmer agree with the ratings ?

Note that when food is plentiful birds will seek food in other places if there is any quarrelling.

During hard winters, however, when food is short, the losers in the quarrels often die. Then during the next summer when there is more food to be shared, the surviving birds tend to have larger families, or fewer young perish. In this way the population is constantly adjusted.

The following graph appeared in the classroom display of some eleven-year-old children in a village school after they examined records kept by the warden of a nearby nature reserve. (1962–3 was a particularly cold winter.)

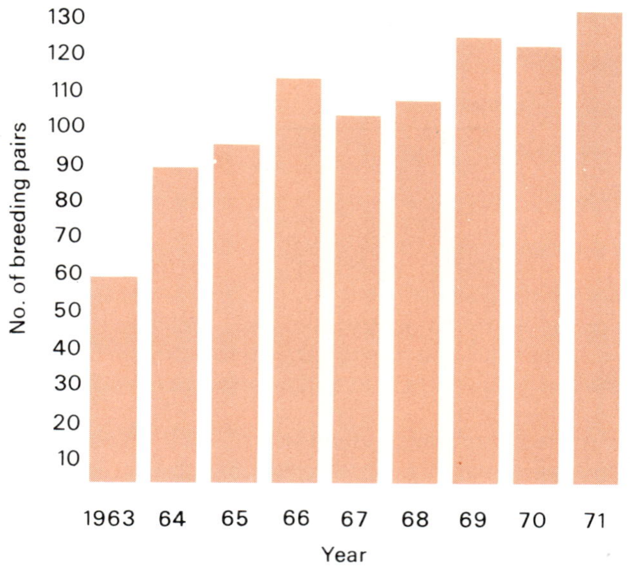

Water predators

If a great diving beetle (*Dytiscus marginalis*) is placed in an aquarium with some of its natural food, for example a dense population of water fleas, it will soon be seen that it is a voracious hunter. In a day or two the water will be clear.

What about the competition between hunters and hunted in a pond? The larger space could make it easier for the water fleas to escape, but there are also likely to be more predatory animals on the prowl such as dragon-fly and *Dytiscus* larvae, water scorpions, water boatmen and sticklebacks.

Water-beetle larva making a capture

Nocturnal predators

Owls hunt at night. They leave clues about their captures since indigestible parts of the creatures they swallow are crushed together and then regurgitated in the form of owl pellets. These can often be found beneath a tree that an owl uses as a roosting place. They repay examination.

To dissect an owl pellet:

Soak it in cold water containing some disinfectant which softens the material and destroys bacteria. Remove surplus water with blotting paper, then place it on a sheet of white paper. Tease the matted fur apart with dissecting needles. Pick the small bones out with fine forceps. Place small drops of colourless glue in rows on black card and lower a skull or bone on to each drop. Put similar bones together on the same line.

One tawny owl's pellet found by some children contained five skulls and ten halves of lower jawbones. Some owls feed on insects and so their pellets contain the chitinous remains of their wing cases, legs and claws.

Examining owl pellets

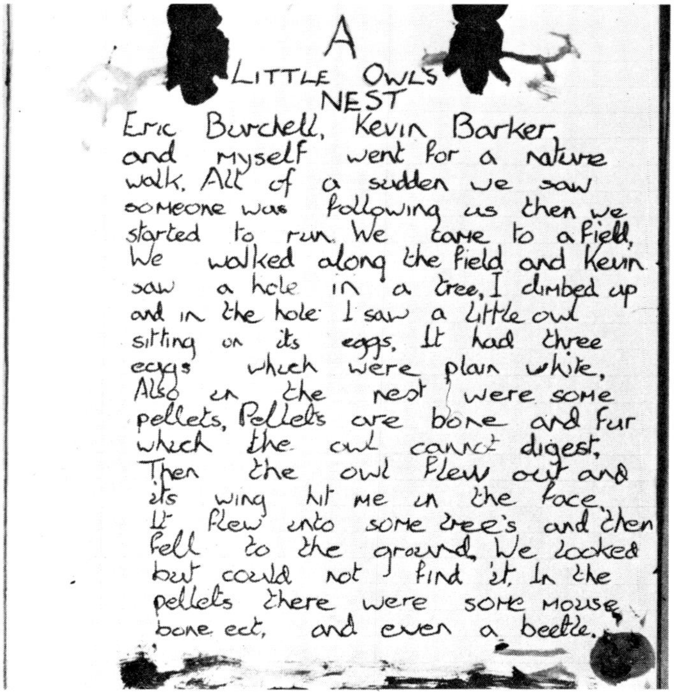

A LITTLE OWLS NEST

Eric Burchell, Kevin Barker, and myself went for a nature walk. All of a sudden we saw someone was following us then we started to run. We came to a field. We walked along the field and Kevin saw a hole in a tree, I climbed up and in the hole I saw a little owl sitting on its eggs. It had three eggs which were plain white. Also in the nest were some pellets, Pellets are bone and fur which the owl cannot digest. Then the owl flew out and its wing hit me in the face. It flew into some tree's and then fell to the ground. We looked but could not find it. In the pellets there were some mouse bone ect, and even a beetle.

Food chains

The competition for life between an owl and its prey, resulting in the capture or escape of the prey, is only one of the happenings in a chain of events. As soon as children begin to suspect this, they may ask: 'What do the animals forming an owl's food live on?' 'Are owls ever attacked and used as food?'

Where does the story of one creature's dependence on another for food begin and end? Can you discover a food chain involving aphids and ladybirds? Keep some in a cage with fresh rose twigs for food and try to find out what happens.

When children attempt further to discover which animals do the eating and which are eaten, they will soon find out that the idea of a feeding chain is an over-simplification. Some predators capture a variety of animals for their prey. Some creatures are in constant danger from a number of different predators. Thus the idea of a feeding web is more appropriate.

Discoveries of interdependence in the school grounds

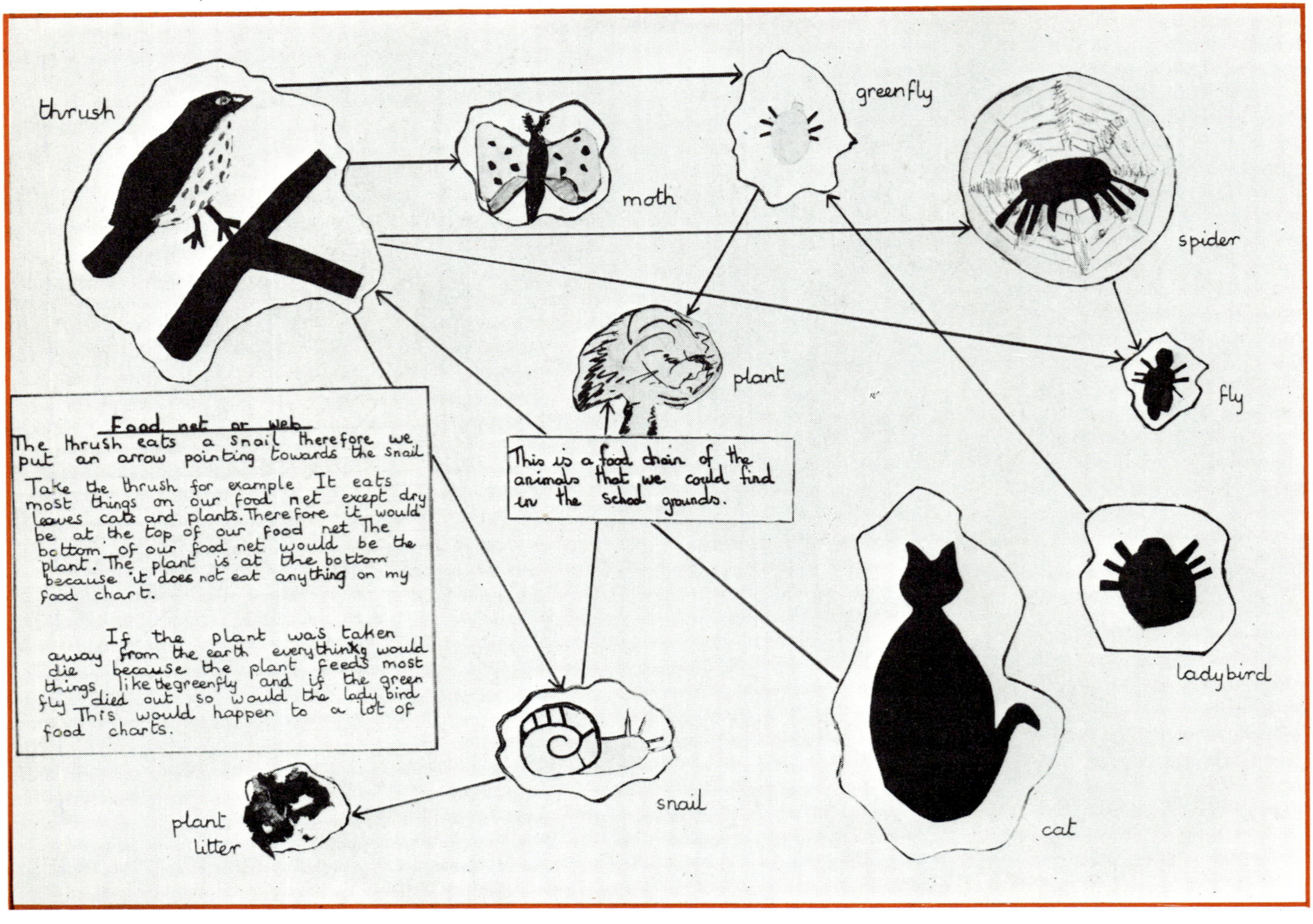

Parasites
Fungi
Where are the best places to look for bracket fungi?
Can you find some wild grasses affected by rust fungus?
What is affecting these leaves?

Is a fungus damaging these leaves?

A stem parasite
During an expedition to some chalk scrubland look for a small plant, the dodder, with pale pink flowers and no leaves twining round bushes.

Later examine it under a stereomicroscope. How does it attach itself to a twig? Does the method of attachment suggest a way in which it might get its food, for it has no green leaves where this can be manufactured?

Such a plant is a parasite living at the expense of the host plant to which it is attached.

The presence of a parasite may lessen the host's power of producing fruits and seeds.

Some plant parasites to look for are:

Eyebright on chalk downland.
Toothwort } in woodland.
Broom rape }

A plant parasite, dodder, growing on wheat

Ichneumons and caterpillars
In September the caterpillars of the cabbage white butterfly may be very common. Collect as many as you can and keep them on a supply of fresh cabbage leaves.

Do they all become chrysalids?
Do some caterpillars die? Examine the sides of any dead caterpillars very carefully.
If you should find a yellow mass attached to a caterpillar, examine your discovery with the help of a stereomicroscope and also look inside the dead caterpillar's skin. What do you think has happened?

Ichneumon-flies often pierce the eggs of cabbage white butterflies on cabbage leaves with the sharp tubes (ovipositors) on the ends of their abdomens. They pass their own eggs down this tube into the butterfly eggs. The ichneumon eggs become larvae inside these eggs which eventually become caterpillars. They feed on the caterpillar hosts until both are ready for pupation. Ichneumon larvae then emerge through the side of the caterpillar and become a mass of cocoons still very close to the host, but by this time the caterpillar is nothing but an empty skin.

Sometimes a caterpillar can be observed as the ichneumon parasites are emerging.

Observe the amount of cabbage leaves being eaten when caterpillars are plentiful.

What would happen if there were no checks on these caterpillars?

Are ichneumon-flies harmful or useful insects?

A caterpillar destroyed by ichneumon larvae

Some other relationships

Children need experience through which they can discover that relationships between two or more living things need not involve the destruction of one thing by another.

Some children between the ages of nine and ten in a small village school near Canterbury made a count of butterflies sighted in their neighbourhood between 28 March and 9 May one year. They recorded 40 cabbage whites, 13 brimstones, 42 peacocks, 51 red admirals and 38 tortoiseshells. Since they kept no records during their Easter holidays, their sample probably indicates a lower population than actually existed during that period.

Butterflies use juices from flowers for food, so the children were also encouraged to consider where this could be obtained by the insects. The village was surrounded by large fruit farms and for much of that time the fruit trees were in blossom and flowers were appearing in many gardens.

The children often visited woods and marshland near their school and the following record of wild flowers observed during the period of the butterfly count has been extracted from the class wild flower chart.

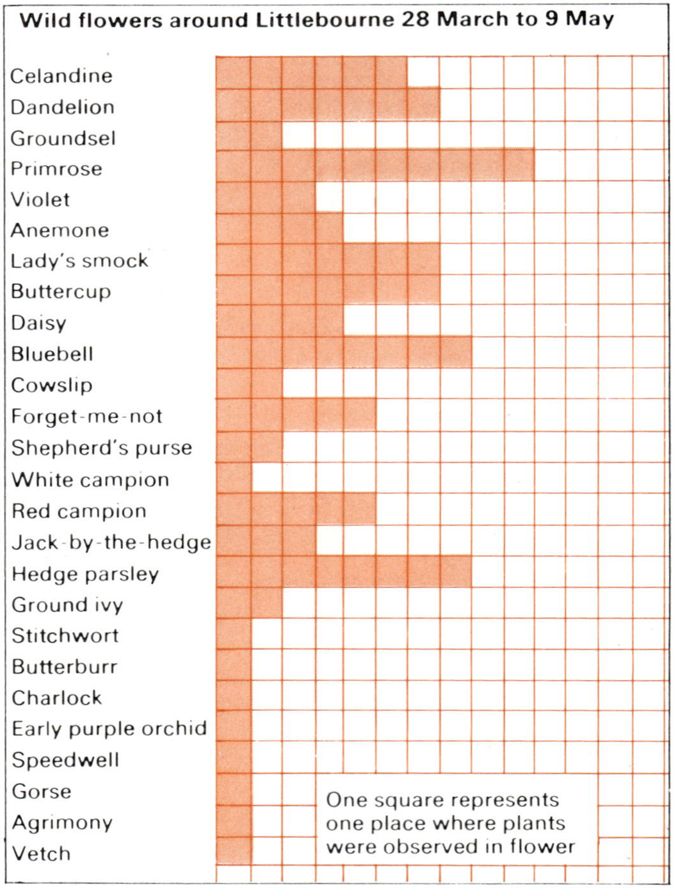

Butterflies actually help plants to grow and spread because when they visit flowers for nectar they are also likely to transfer pollen from one flower to another, thus assisting the production of fruit and seed.

Butterflies are also themselves the food of insect-eating birds. Their edibility helps some birds to survive.

Birds, and other animals, act as agents for the dispersal of fruit and seed.

Plant growth demonstrates how in a given spot some seeds will find good conditions for growth. One effect of this may be that other plants will be eliminated from the habitat because of overcrowding. On the other hand, certain animals may appear there because the food plants they require become available, for instance, the cinnabar moth which lives on ragwort.

Children can discover through their investigations many relationships between living things. Some work towards the increase of a species, others towards depletion. The experience will help them to begin to realise that living things continually affect each other ; that, in other words, they are interdependent.

A class of children might try to illustrate this fundamental concept with a corporate piece of work. They could make an expedition to some waste ground or another suitable place within reach of the school. While they are there they should draw a large sketch of the place. Back in the classroom each child should study the plants or small creatures they have collected and make careful drawings of them. Then the drawings could be attached to the sketch in positions corresponding to the places where the animals or plants were found. Finally, the children could indicate any relationships they think they have discovered by connecting appropriate pairs with coloured pencil lines or tapes. These activities will stimulate much discussion and vigorous argument, and consequently much thought. They may even reach the stage of asking what would happen if there were no plants.

A way in which children might record their discoveries about relationships between living things

Growth of a broad bean

The primary root appears

The root lengthens and the shoot appears

Secondary roots are appearing rapidly

Vigorous growth of whole root system

3 Discovering relationships between form and function in plants: roots, stems, leaves

What is it there for? Has it any use? These may seem like obvious questions, perhaps, as children observe a shoot unfolding, but how often are they recognised also as starting points for some very valuable experience?

The many useful purposes served by the various parts of living things can only be determined by careful studies of cells and organs and experimental techniques beyond the capacity of twelve-year-old children. There are, however, simpler investigations through which they can begin to discover 'how things work' as well as 'what they are like'. These will be our concern in this chapter.

A good stereomagnifier is again required, because many of the parts of living things the children will need to examine are small.

If much of the material required for first-hand examination and testing can be found or grown in the school garden, there will be less danger of over-collecting from the countryside.

Roots

Roots as anchors

This study could begin when a flower bed requires weeding, or carrots and lettuce need thinning.

When is the best time for tackling these jobs? Soon after rain or during a dry sunny spell? In what condition does the soil have to be to hold plants more firmly? Does water in the soil serve as a lubricant?

What about the roots of the plants that have been removed? Are they all the same, or different?

Were some plants harder to pull up than others?

While the work is progressing, sort the plants into three piles consisting of:

Those removed by gentle pulls.
Those requiring strong steady pulls to remove them.
Those with the root system broken through being pulled out.

A classroom display of different types of roots would be useful at this stage.

Begin preparing material for this by washing the uprooted plants. Agitate their roots in a bowl of water and gently brush away soil particles with an old paint brush. (Do not pour this muddy water down a sink.)

Find some roots used for food. A look in the greengrocer's shop window may help. (You should find carrots, parsnip, beetroot.)

Search for plants with roots growing from various parts of the stems (ivy, creeping buttercup, iris).

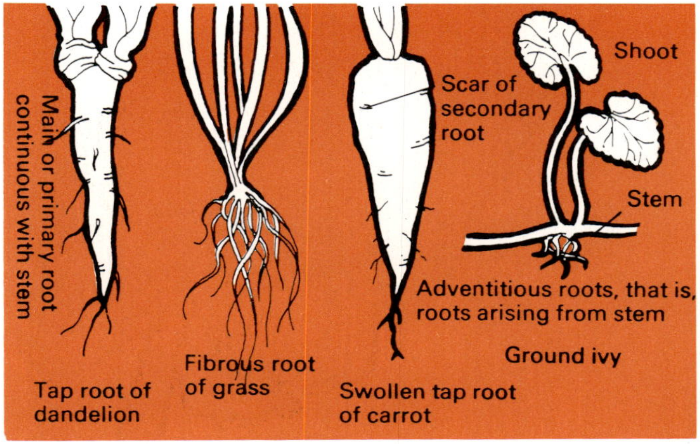

While children are arranging and labelling the specimens collected through these activities their teacher can find many opportunities to associate appropriate vocabulary with particular roots.

Can roots be made to grow from leaves?
Try to produce a number of plants from a large begonia leaf. There are two ways of doing this.

1. Make some cuts across the main veins on the back of the leaf.

Press the base of the leaf stalk into a seed tray containing compost made by mixing equal parts by volume of peat and sand.

Then make sure that all cuts across the veins are in contact with the compost and maintain them in that position by placing small pebbles on the leaf.

Small plants will appear at the points where the veins were cut. These can be transferred to individual pots when they have reached a suitable size.

2. Divide the begonia leaf into small squares. Make sure that each of them contains a strong vein.

Place the squares on the compost so that their under-surfaces are in contact with it. Hold the pieces in place with small pebbles.

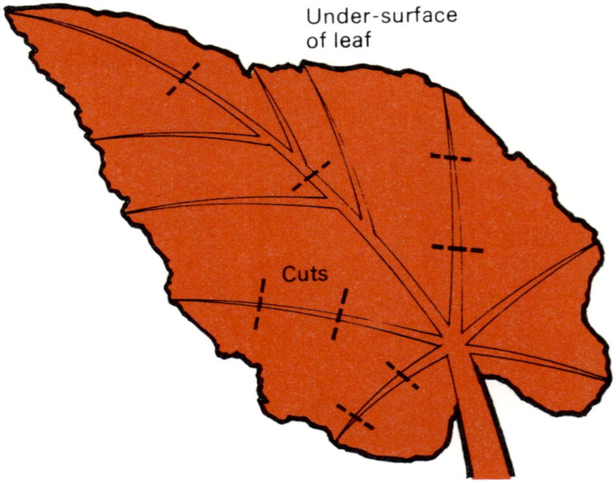

The development of the root system
The development of the root system in relation to the soil could be closely examined. (See page 30.)

Fill a wormery with John Innes seed compost. Place a soaked broad bean or pea seed between the compost and one of the glass sides of the wormery, about 2 cm below the compost's surface. Keep it supplied with sufficient water.

As children observe this development they may be able to make suggestions about what makes roots become more efficient anchoring systems as the plant grows.

For example:

1. Downward growth.

Can roots be made to grow in any other direction?
Try rotating growing plants in a germination sandwich. (See Volume 2 Part 2, page 25.)

2. The penetration of increasing numbers of secondary roots between soil particles.

3. The increasing size of swollen tap roots.

Does this make them fit more tightly into the space they occupy in the soil?

Measuring anchoring power
In order to make better comparisons of the anchoring power of different root systems, children must devise a way of measuring the strength of pulls required to remove plants from the soil.

Tie a series of a few half hitches round a plant, beginning at the bottom, at ground level.

Tighten the knot and tie a loop in the free end of the string. Attach a newton-meter to the loop and exert a steady pull.

The strength of pulls required to uproot plants can be read from the newton-meter.

Sometimes the extension of a rubber band can serve as an arbitrary measure.

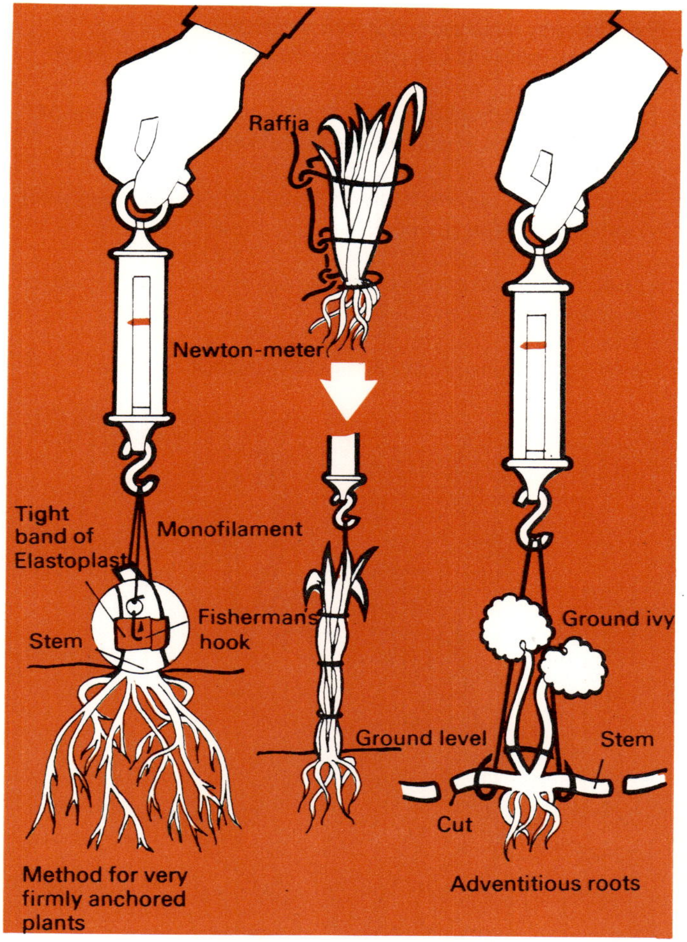

Methods of attaching a newton-meter for measuring the anchoring power of roots

Children can use these tests to try to discover which of the following makes root systems better anchoring devices :

The increasing outward spread, eg in beans, peas.
The increasing length and thickness of the main root, eg in sea holly, hogweed, dandelion, bindweed.
The increasing mass of the tap root, eg in carrots, turnips.
The increasing number of adventitious roots, eg in creeping buttercup, couch-grass, iris, stinging nettle.

They can also try to find out the force of pull required to uproot plants from wet and dry soil ; and from different soils, such as sand, clay, peat, etc.

Children in schools near seashores may become interested in the anchoring power of seaweed holdfasts.

The planning of these comparisons will give children opportunities of considering which conditions must be kept similar, and which can be ignored.

Does anchoring power increase with growth ?
Here is a way of finding out.

Soak about thirty broad bean seeds. Ask each child to attach a loop to one seed by boring a hole through its thickest part, passing a length of raffia through it and knotting it.

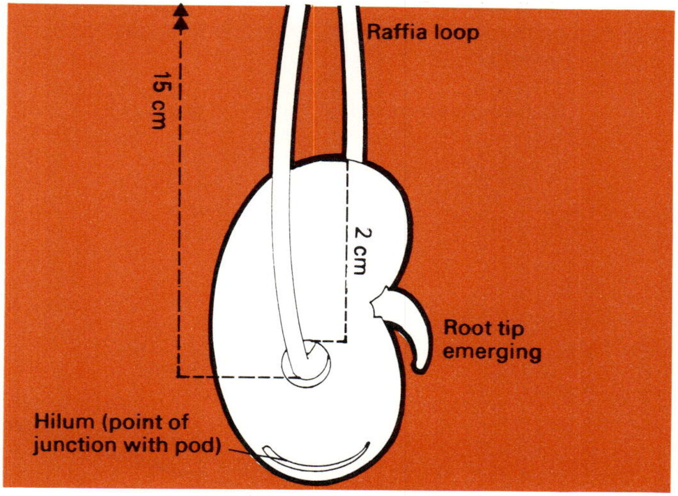

Prepare a seed bed in the school garden. Sow five of the prepared beans in the bed 10 cm apart and 2 cm deep with the raffia loops protruding from the soil and held vertical by twine as in the next picture.

After six days attach newton-meters to the loops of the seeds and find the average strength of pulls required to remove them from the soil.

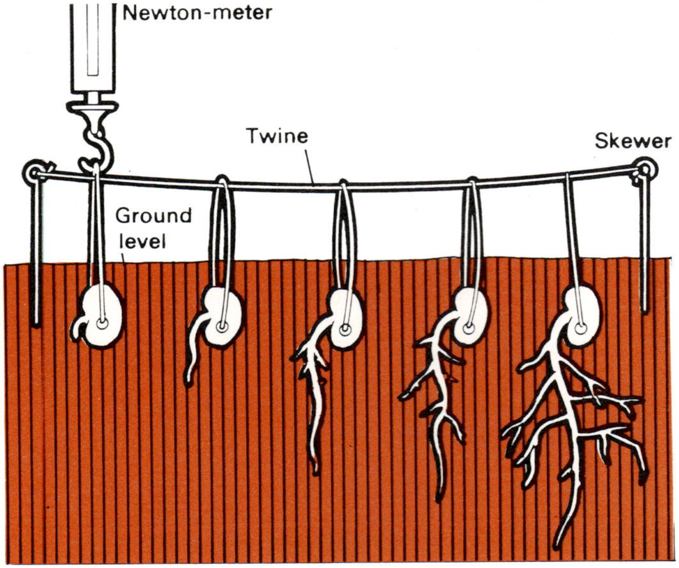

Repeat using five seeds each time and pull up these batches on the 9th, 12th, 15th, 18th and 21st days after sowing the first batch.

Record of results of test shown on graph

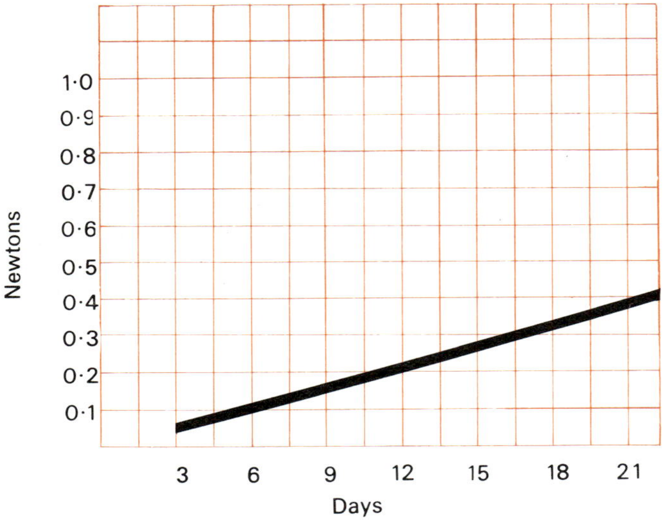

Roots as collectors of water

What happens if we change the surroundings of roots?

Carrots or weeds of the same species at similar stages of development are suitable plants for comparisons.

Uproot some specimens and suspend them at convenient heights above the ground.

At two-hourly intervals compare them with similar plants growing naturally in the soil.

Do some of these plants wilt owing to lack of water?

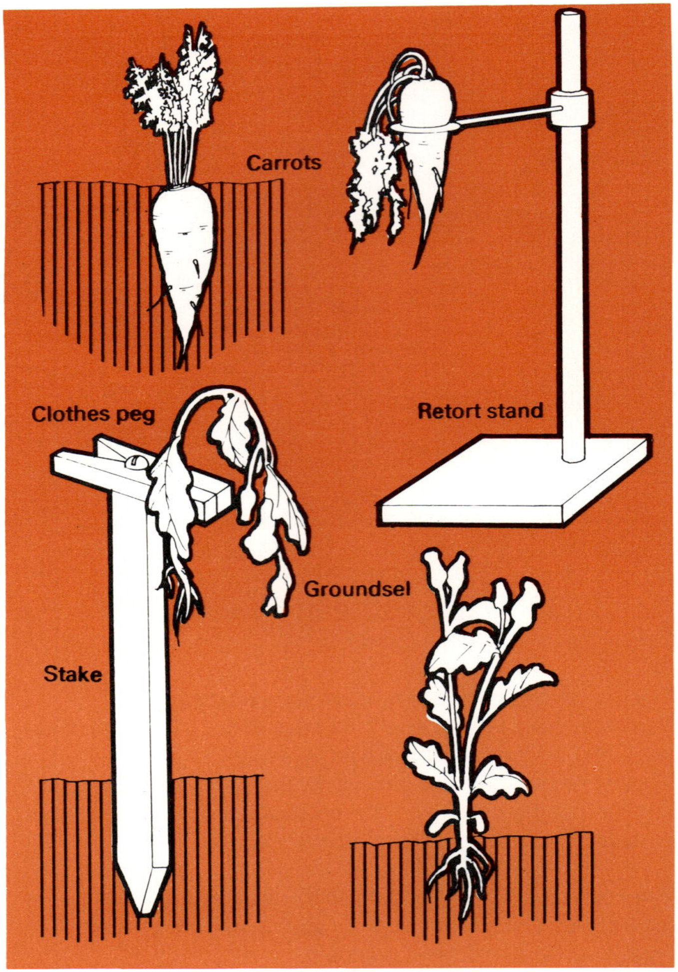

Here is another comparison to illustrate the relationship of roots to the water supplies around them.

What part of the plant in bottle no. 1 is in contact with the water supply ?

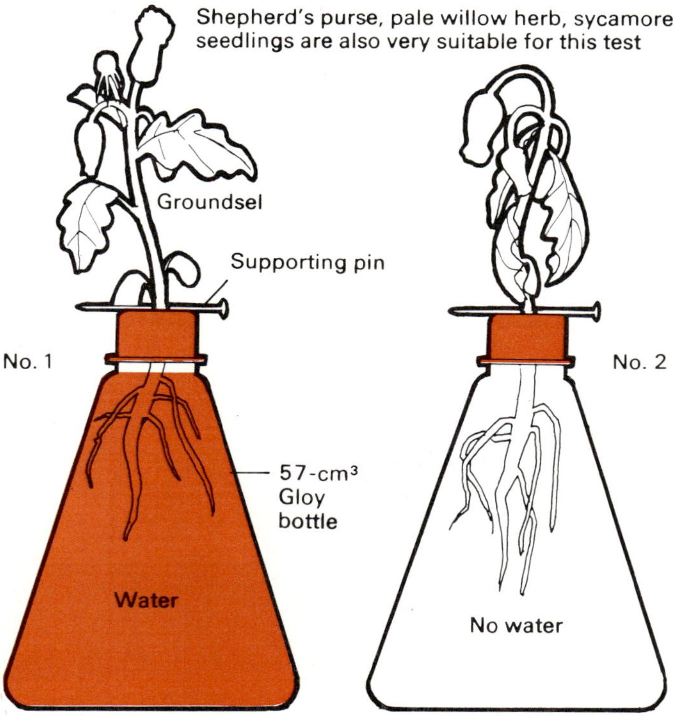

Can we make water pass in and out of roots ?
Hollow out the centres of three carrot roots of similar size and place water and a strong sugar solution in relation to them as shown here. Make careful drawings showing the water levels at the beginning of the investigation.

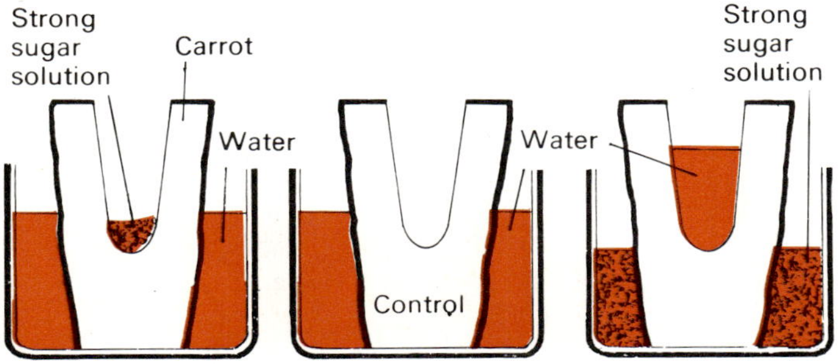

Compare the water levels after three hours with the drawings made at the beginning of the investigation.

Perhaps liquids (sap) in roots draw water from the soil towards themselves, as sugar solution seems to do here ?

Do larger root systems collect more water for plants than smaller ones ?
The inverted plastic caps of 57-cm^3 Gloy bottles are convenient holders for germinating peas, and the bottles can serve as reservoirs for the water required by the seeds during this investigation. The peas in bottles should be set up at four-day intervals.

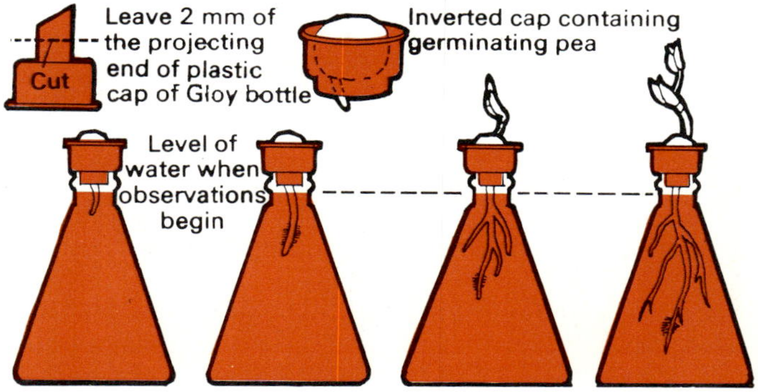

When you have set up four peas in bottles and four root systems of different sizes have been produced, top up the water so that the levels in all the bottles are immediately below the plastic caps.

At the same time each day for the next week mark the level of water in each bottle.

Roots as collectors of another material

Soak some peas in water until their roots begin to emerge.

Again using plastic caps to hold them, fill some of the Gloy bottles with distilled water and others with tap or rainwater to which a liquid chemical fertiliser such as Kerigrow has been added in the proportion of 5 ml to 0·57 litre (1 pint).

Compare the growth of the shoots of these plants.

If plants with roots in water and fertiliser produce a better growth, this provides some evidence that chemicals dissolved in water are also entering plant roots.

Stems

Stems as supports

Think of all the different positions occupied by the leaves and flowers on a horse chestnut tree in full bloom, or on different plants in a hedgerow at the height of summer. What holds up each one of these things in its own place ?

Stems, trunks, branches and leaf stalks must be strong enough to remain erect or extended sideways for this purpose.

What structure provides this strength ?
In trees and shrubs the answer to this question is, obviously, wood. Have a good look at some surfaces of tree stumps and some cut surfaces of branches. How much of the stem consists of wood ?

Measure the distances between neighbouring rings of growth. Is the same amount added each year ?

Are all the woody parts of tree trunks equally strong ? Try hardness tests from the heart and sap wood of the same tree. (See Volume 2 Part 1, page 68 for an appropriate test.)

The dead parts of plants such as sorrel, dock, teasel and hogweed form beautiful shapes and patterns in the country in the winter. Their supporting parts will still be there for us to examine.

Patterns against the sky made by hogweed in winter

Look at the cut end of a piece of hogweed stem with the aid of a stereomicroscope. Split a piece about 6 cm long in halves lengthwise. Scrape out the pith from the centre of one half. What remains ? How would you describe it ? Could it serve as a means of support ?

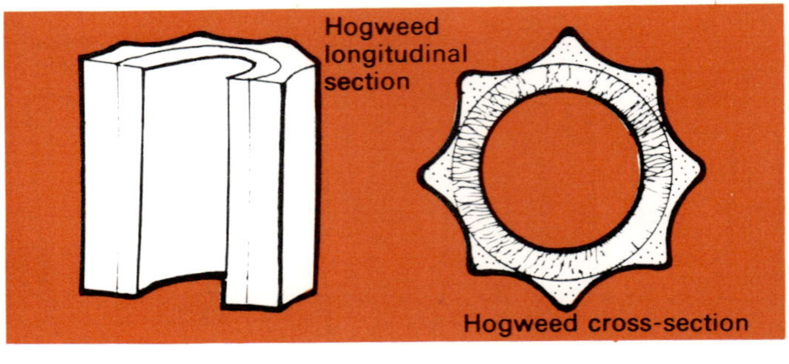

Try to strip some fibres from the tough old stems of rhubarb or celery. Leave an old cabbage stalk out of doors in water to rot, and then rinse away the remains of the softer decayed parts. Examine the tougher parts left with the help of a stereomagnifier. What are they like?

Straw and bamboo are the supporting parts of stems that we put to other uses. From what group of plants are they obtained? (Grasses.)

Now try to find the hardest material running the length of stems that are not woody. Strip off the green outermost layer. Cut pieces lengthwise and scrape away any soft pith they may contain. What remains? What position does this harder strengthening material seem to occupy in stems?

Does any particular shape appear to be common to the strengthening material in trees and herbaceous plants? (The cylinder.)

An examination of straw shows that the layer of supporting material in grasses is much thinner than in many plants.

Examine some living grasses and try to find an arrangement that provides additional support. Can this device be found in any other plants?

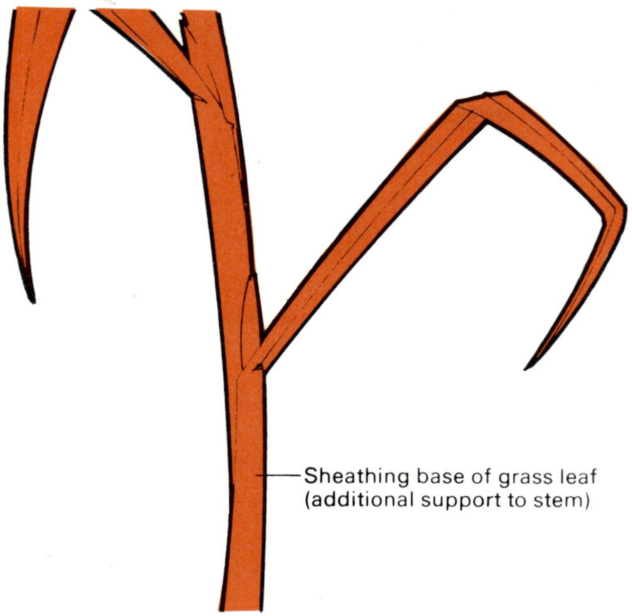

Children will have had plenty of experience of finding out that plants that are not woody soon stop being erect when they are deprived of water.

Compare two sets of similar plants. It is important to make sure they are all the same height when you set up the test.

The cells of plants in water become very tightly packed with water and the push of the cell wall opposing the force exerted by water in the opposite direction holds the stem upright. If water is removed then its opposing force obviously lessens and the plant becomes less rigid.

Do some plants wilt more rapidly than others? By timing the wilting rates of different plants children may be able to discover more about the contribution made by water to the support of these plants. For how long can various plants remain in a wilting condition before failing to recover when supplied with water?

Comparing stems

We have seen that stems must be strong and rigid to support other parts of plants. However it is only necessary to observe plants in a strong wind to discover the advantage of stems that can bend and then return to their original positions. We need to carry out some tests in order to find out whether different stems show much variation in strength and pliability.

Strength tests

1. For stems of herbaceous plants.

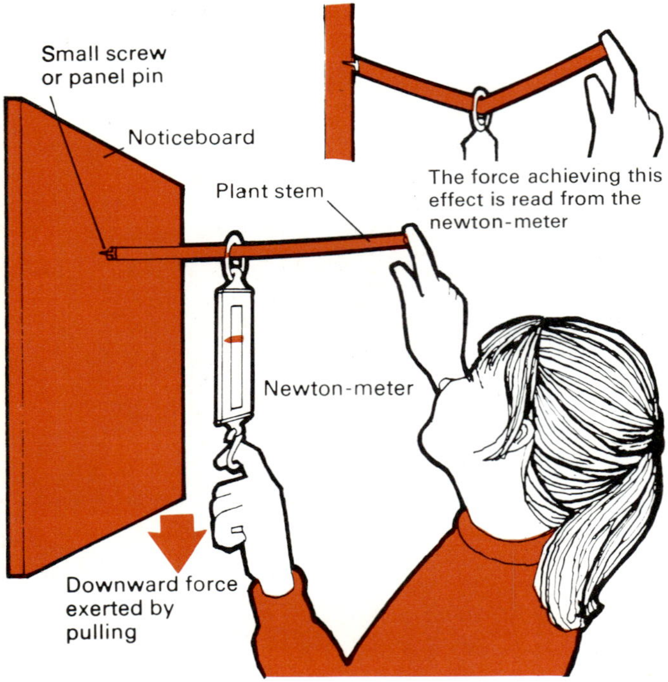

A rubber band can be used instead of the newton-meter, and the increase in its length as the stem bends may be taken as an arbitrary measure.

2. See Volume 2 Part 1, page 69 for a method of testing the strength of thick, woody stems.

A test for pliability

How far can the free end of the stem be pushed downwards before breaking? Does it always return to its original position if it is released before the breaking point is reached?

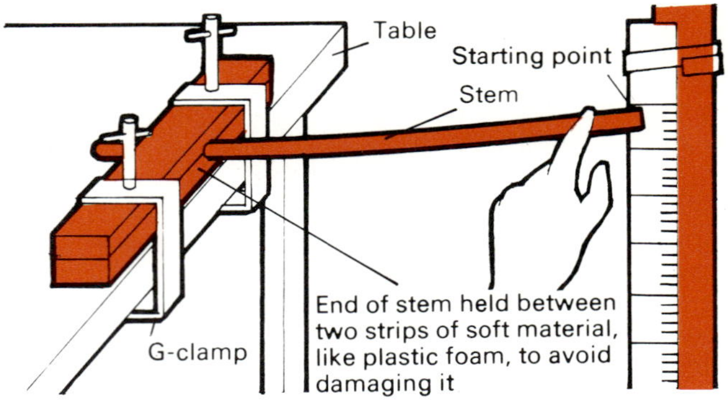

Children may find good reasons for using these tests when they make comparisons of the following types of stems:

1. Thick and thin ones.
2. Hollow and solid ones.
3. Stems of different shape in cross-section.

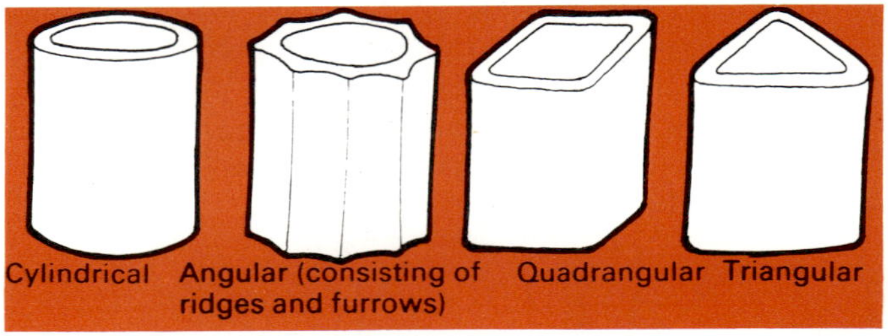

4. Green living and dry dead lengths of stem from the same plant. These can be found on hawthorn and sycamore.
5. Long and short lengths of the same stem. What sort of plants need to be tied to stakes in the garden?

Again children must be encouraged to think about conditions. They must be comparable for tests to be fair.

Weak stems

There is no doubt that leaves and flowers attached to weak stems manage to reach positions where they can obtain plenty of light or attract pollinating insects.

If children have not made any studies of the way weakness or lack of supporting material in certain stems is overcome this is a good time to do so. They will find the same problem solved in different ways.

A branch distorted by twining honeysuckle

Climbing plants can be found attached to self-supporting plants by twisting stems and leaf stalks, modified leaves, adventitious roots, suckers and hooked structures. This is interesting. Does this sort of thing often happen? What about trying to find other examples of achieving the same result? (See pages 60–61.)

These stems may provide weak support but they can exert pressure.

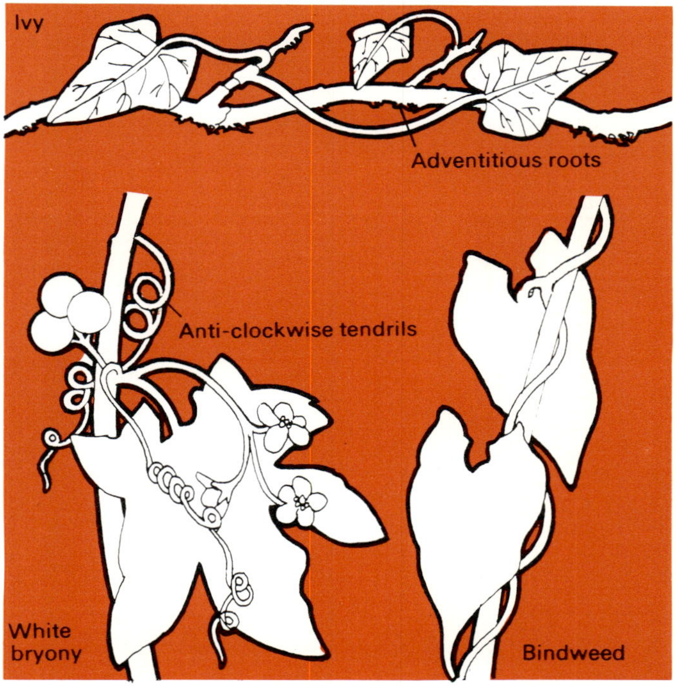

In the course of their explorations children will come across stems that are not upright. This will cause much discussion.

Here are some examples:

Creeping buttercup, ground ivy — what happens at each node on these stems?
Dandelion, plantain, daisy — why do the leaves on these stems form rosettes?
Solomon's seal, iris — where are the stems of these plants? What are they called?
Couch grass — why is this plant a persistent weed?

Routes for moving water

Where do water and any dissolved materials that may be drawn into the roots of a plant go? Do they go everywhere?

Groups of children could look at some uprooted weeds.

When they have found out which parts of their plants join on to each other, they could try to produce plans of routes that the water might take.

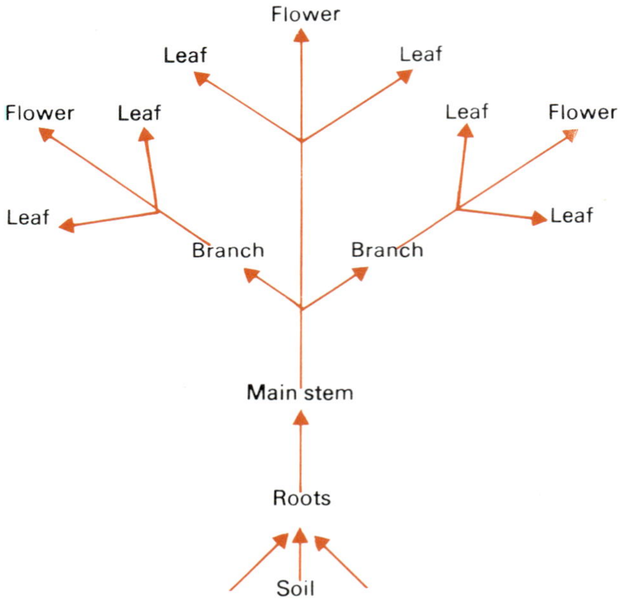

Then the children must search for evidence to support their ideas. The water must be traced; this is easier if it is coloured.

Here are some colouring materials that the children might add to water or use undiluted:

Chemical dyes—eosin (red ink), methylene blue.
Food colouring liquids—cochineal, proprietary brands.
Coloured plant juices—beetroot, blackcurrant, which should be crushed or shredded when raw and soaked in water.

Does water reach all the parts of a plant?

Children should try various combinations of coloured water and plants, that is:

The same plants in different coloured liquids.
Different plants in the same coloured liquids.

It is important to use complete plants for this test, so that children may collect evidence of a continuous route from roots to leaves and flowers. The green colouring in plants may make some colours difficult to distinguish.

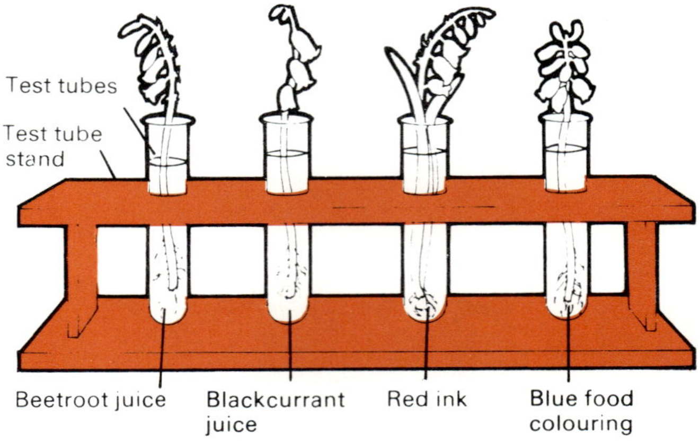

Grow sets of mustard plants on cottonwool dampened with differently coloured liquids. Keep them in a dark place to prevent green colouring forming.

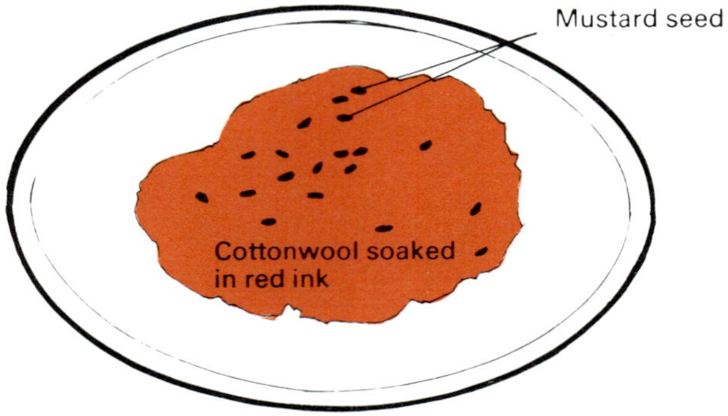

Are any of the coloured liquids taken up by these plants? Children will probably find that red ink provides the most convincing demonstration of how water passes through plants.

Does the water travelling through plants follow any special routes?

Plant material lacking much colour is the best for these investigations, such as:

Leaf stalks of celery with some leaves attached.
Daisies, white carnations, narcissi flowers.
White and pale pink clematis flowers.

When children get results, they will become interested in testing many other specimens and parts of plants.

What suggestions could children make if they obtain this result when they cut across and lengthwise celery stems they have left in red ink?

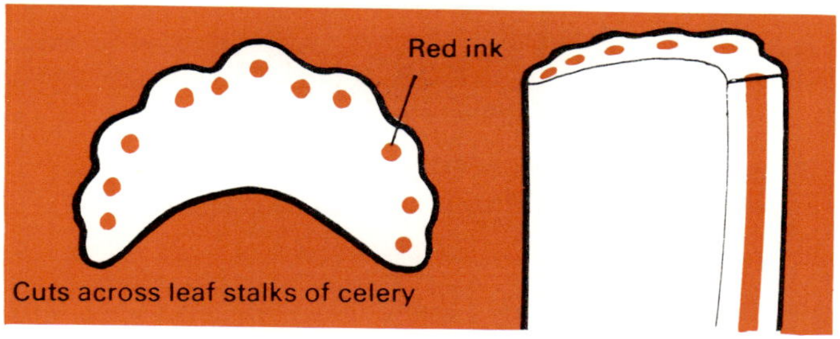

The branching network of tubes or veins extending over every part of leaves and flower petals can be seen very, effectively when leaf skeletons are examined, or if a pale clematis flower is placed with its stem in red ink for a short time.

These tubes also provide some support for the plant tissue. Their persistence in leaf skeletons is further evidence of their toughness.

Do liquids pass from the water tubes to other parts of the plants?

A comparison of two clematis petals, one from a flower in water and the other from a flower left in red ink for a rather longer period than normal for testing, shows how the dye gradually accumulates in all parts of a petal. Similar results can also be obtained with leaves.

Children can carry out some interesting investigations into the time colouring takes to reach various parts of different plants.

Leaves

In and out of leaves

We have found that water gets into leaves, and we have found some of the tubes along which it travels. Is it possible to collect any evidence that water can also get out?

Tie plastic bags round some leaves growing on various plants in the school grounds. Make sure that no part of the leaf stalk is included.

Examine at intervals throughout the day. Repeat the investigation using similar leaves for the same length of time during different weather conditions, such as dull, sunny, chilly, warm. Are there any occasions when water appears to be collecting more rapidly in the plastic bag?

Does the mass of a leaf change as it withers? What could a decrease in mass suggest? Do different weather conditions affect the rate of this change?

Is water lost from both sides of a leaf?

Take three large tough leaves, such as laurel. Cover with a layer of Vaseline both surfaces of one, the upper surface of another, and the under surface of the third. Now hang these leaves on similar drinking-straw balances and note whether any change in mass takes place in any specimen. Loss of water from a leaf could cause a loss in mass.

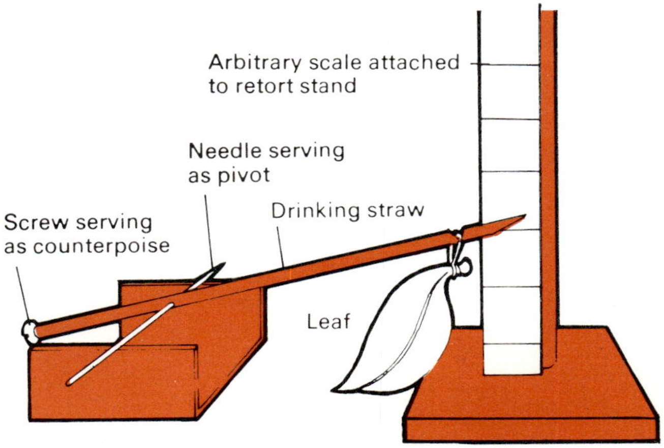

Is it possible to find any exits in leaves?
Insert the point of a dissecting needle under the thin outer surface of the leaf of an iris or onion. Work it gently about until a strip of material becomes detached. Then obtain a similar strip from the other side of the leaf. Mount these strips in water on microscope slides and examine them carefully using the highest powered lens of the stereomagnifier. If a monocular microscope is available, use that too for examining this material. (The word 'stomata' can be introduced when an exit is discovered.)

Leaf cuticle magnified to show stomata surrounded by guard cells

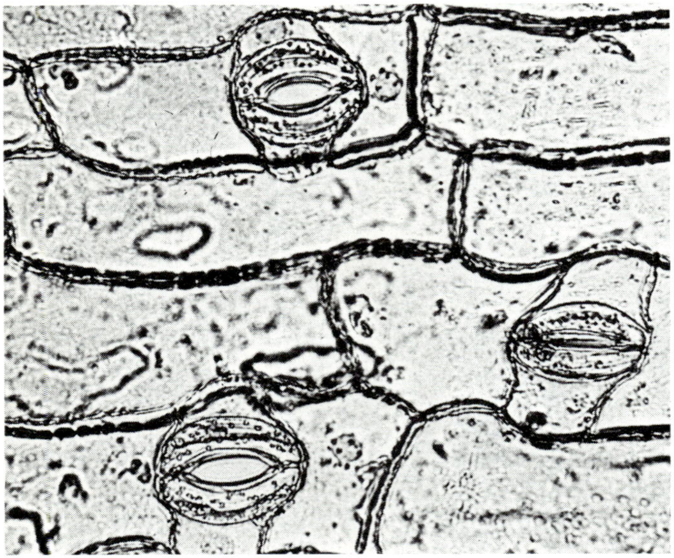

Is water the only substance that gets out of leaves?
Lower some freshly picked leaves into a beaker of hot water.

Can anything be seen emerging from one or both of the leaf surfaces?

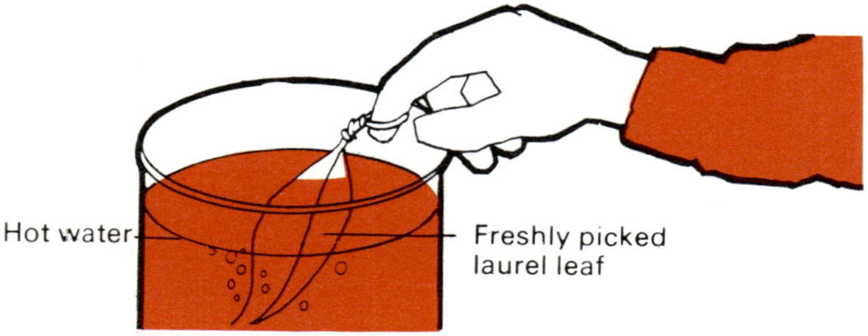

Does whatever appears seem to be coming from exits corresponding in position to the stomata?

Here is a demonstration that can be used as a basis for discussion.

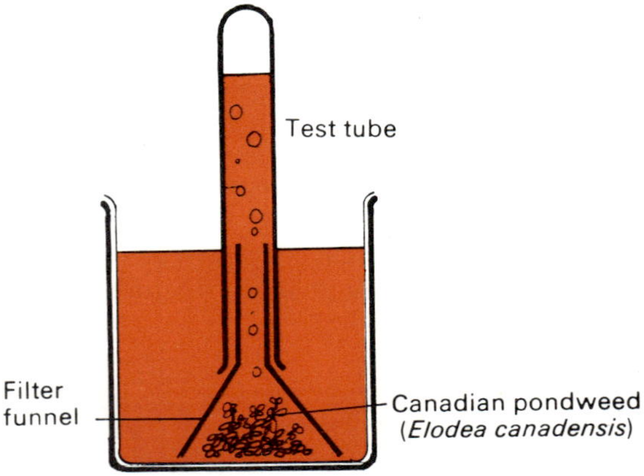

Does anything come from the plant leaves? Does this appear at any time or only under certain weather conditions?

If children have had any experience of oxygen and carbon dioxide they can try testing the gas accumulating in the test-tube, but if not they can simply decide that an invisible gas comes out of the leaves.

It should be suggested to the children that if gases can get out of leaves it is also possible that they can enter by the same openings.

However, an investigation of what happens to raw materials that get into leaves, ie photosynthesis, will be more appropriate at a later stage (see Nuffield *Biology Year 3*).

Children should keep on observing the following characteristics of leaves:

Their flatness.
The tendency of their upper surfaces to face the source of light.
Their mosaic arrangement when on a tree so that many get a share of the strongest light.
The relationship between light and their greenness.

These observations, together with searching for evidence of ways in which materials get in and out of leaves, will be good experience on which to base more advanced studies.

Modified leaves

On many occasions, as children investigate leaves, they will probably find evidence that some are very different from the ordinary green foliage type and are obviously of different uses.

Try to obtain some seeds of the yellow vetchling (*Lathyrus aphaca*) or sweet pea (*Lathyrus odoratus*). Plant near a trellis in the school garden.

How does this plant attach itself to the trellis as it grows taller?

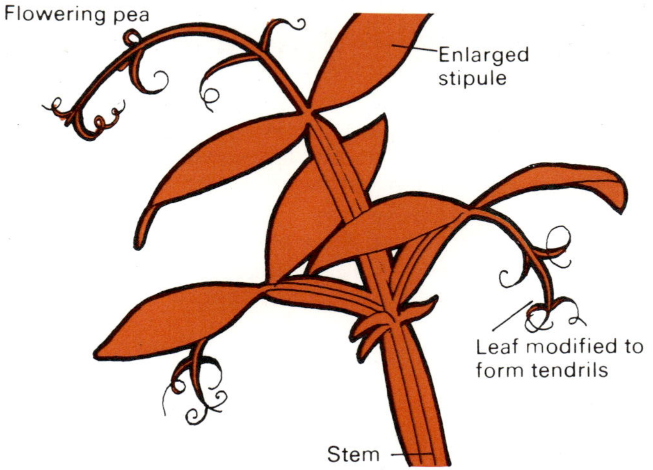

In some plants pairs of small leaf-like structures can be found at the bases of leaf stalks where they join the stem. These are stipules.

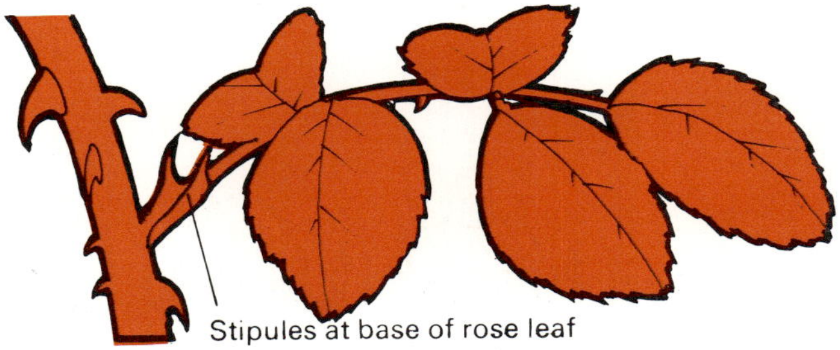

A convincing demonstration of stages in the modification of leaves from their original form to something serving another purpose can be found in seedlings of gorse (*Ulex europaeus*).

Search for some of these on heathland becoming recolonised after burning. Remove the leaves from a plant and arrange them in sequence according to the position they occupied from base to apex on the stem. Look for stages ranging between flat, trifoliate green leaves and small spines. Larger spines in their axils provide evidence of them being reduced leaves.

Since grazing animals are unlikely to feed on prickly gorse plants, it is reasonable to suppose that the spines protect the plant.

Scale leaves enclose the leaf buds and protect the young leaves and shoots inside. Sepals enclose the flower buds and protect parts of the flower during the early stages of their development.

Can any evidence be found to support these statements?

Are these modified leaves impermeable to water?

Do they bear any structures between which air could be trapped to make insulating layers around young parts? Look on their inner surfaces.

Here the children might be encouraged to think of how birds fluff up their feathers on cold days and how we wear woollen clothing in winter and so make use of air which is a bad conductor of heat and therefore a good insulator.

Can any connection be found between the movement apart of bud scales and sepals and changes in temperature?

Some parts of plants that store food materials

We eat many parts of plants. Are these parts where food materials collect during the growing season?

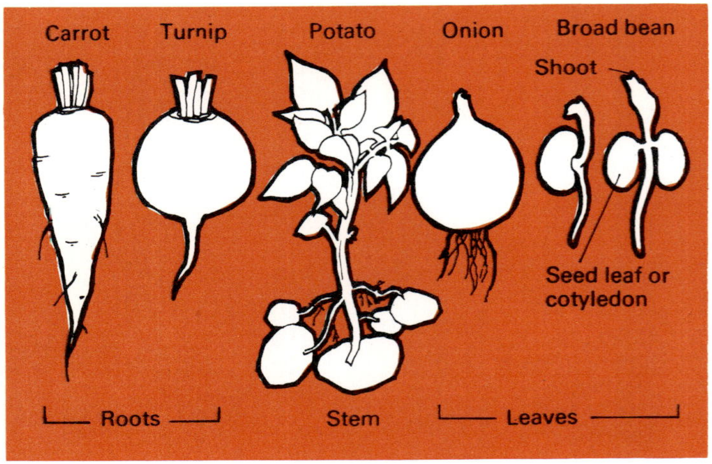

Of what use would these stores of food be to the plant if we did not take them? Children can use carrots to follow up this question.

Here is a record, drawn to scale, of the two-year life cycle.

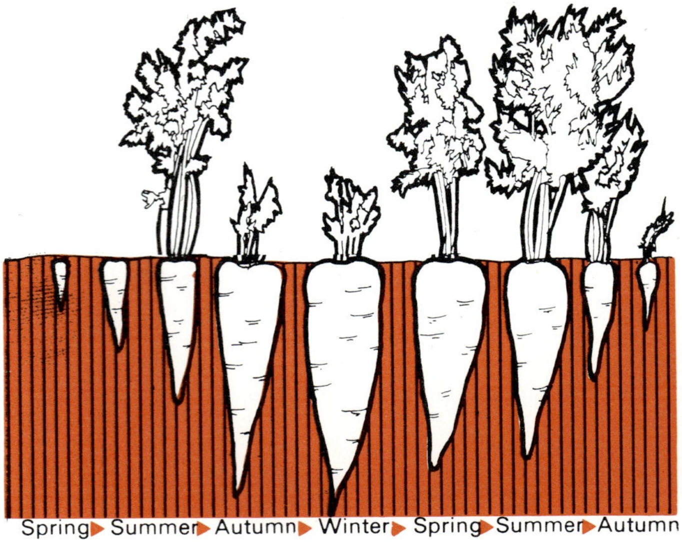

If a stock at different stages of development are always kept in the school gardens, children can dig up specimens and see what is happening to them.

What causes new parts to show above the ground at the beginning of the second growing season? (Growth of buds in the axils of old leaves.)

Where did the material required for starting off the new growth come from?

Further evidence of the use of stored food supplies can be obtained by observing what happens when the tops of swollen roots, a piece of potato containing some eyes and an onion are placed in water. Search for buds from which new shoots might come. Where are the best places to look?

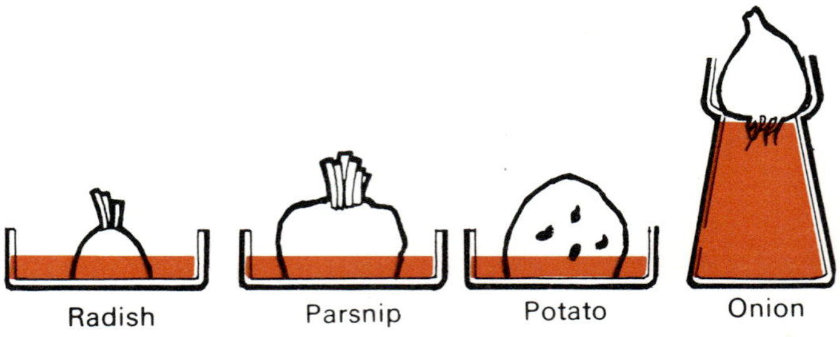

This turnip top gave rise to a new growth of leaves when it was left in water for a few weeks

These investigations suggest that plants requiring more than one growing season to complete their life cycles from seed to seed depend on food stored in swollen parts to stimulate their second season's growth.

In some herbaceous plants, known as perennials, the death of the parts above ground in autumn and the new spring growth from underground organs continues indefinitely. Dandelions, cow parsley and broad dock are common examples.

Do any parts of these plants below ground become larger and thicker in the course of development, suggesting the accumulation of food material ? Dig up some roots and examine them carefully.

Annual plants such as poppies complete their life cycles in one season and then die. Ephemeral plants like groundsel and shepherd's purse have even shorter cycles. Do any roots or stems below ground in these plants become enlarged ? How is the continuity of their species achieved ?

4 Discovering relationships between form and function in plants: flowers, pollen, fruit, seeds

Here children will be working again with some of the parts of plants they are most likely to find familiar, but their problems now will be concerned with whether the colours, shapes and sizes they compared so often in arranging their earlier collections of wild flowers, fruits and seeds have any further significance.

The most suitable time for the investigations suggested in this chapter is from early April to the end of October.

Flowers and insect visitors

By this time children will probably enjoy a much more extensive search than any previously made (see Volume 2 Part 1, page 21 and Volume 3 Part 1, page 19) for relationships between the characteristics of flowers and the number and variety of their insect visitors. This could become a major class activity proceeding along with other studies during the summer term. It will provide excellent experience in planning and carrying out a more sustained study.

A class discussion could be held to start the investigation off.

What information about flowers and their visitors is needed?

Can suggestions be put into questionnaire form?
A sample questionnaire is given on page 47

Before the form of questionnaire can be finally agreed upon, however, certain matters will have to be settled so that the collected information will be as valid as possible.

One important factor that must be taken into account is that children's sight and sense of smell vary. Therefore sight and smelling tests must be devised to be taken by all members of the class.

One test might consist of the ability to see a postcard held at given distances.

200 m — long sight.
100 m — average sight.
Not more than 25 m — short sight.

Another test might consist of the ability to detect the smell of Airwick at given distances.

5 m — keen smelling sense.
2 m — average smelling sense.
Not more than 0·5 m — weak smelling sense.

Children must fill in their own grades on any questionnaire form they complete. Allowance for these grades will be made when the data from the questionnaire are analysed.

A standard method of carrying out visibility tests on flowers must be agreed upon. What background should flowers be viewed against?

Children will probably find it is best to organise themselves into pairs for collecting information. However, each form should be signed by the child who makes the observations on visibility and smelling.

A questionnaire form should be completed for each flower observed (see page 47) and each flower should be observed for the same length of time, such as 15 minutes. It should be completed at different times and in as many places as possible — gardens, parks, waste ground, woods, chalk downland, heathland, etc.

Date of observation	July 4th 1973
Time of observation	12·00 – 12·15 hours
Weather conditions	Hot, Sunny, calm

Name of flower	Hogweed (Heracleum sphondylium)
State:	☐ young ☑ mature ☐ old
Arrangement:	☐ single ☑ many small flowers together
Colour	white
Shape	side from above
Entry to corolla:	☑ easy ☐ difficult
Size viewed from above:	length 10cm width 12cm
Height above ground	1m
Distance visible	158m
Scent:	☐ present ☑ absent
Penetration of scent	

Insect visitors from 12·00 to 12·15 hours:	
Flies	10
Bees	0
Wasps	0
Butterflies, moths	0
Beetles	6
Others	2
Any interesting observations of behaviour during visit	

Observer	Mary Smith
Sense of sight	Long
Sense of smell	Average

It is essential that children should understand that records of observations when *no* insects visit flowers are as important as any others. These occasions may throw light on the effects of certain weather conditions on insect behaviour and will also support the suggestion that certain flowers are not pollinated by insects.

Completed questionnaires should be stored in a class file in the resources area. The more data that are accumulated as time passes the greater will be the value of this file.

Much interesting argument and discussion will arise when groups of children try to find answers to different questions by analysing the results of the survey, for example:

What flower colour seems to be most attractive to insects?
Does the size of flower or inflorescence make much difference?
Which flowers attract by scent rather than appearance?
Which flowers only receive visits from one type of insect?
Do tall plants receive more insect visitors than short ones?
Do all insect visitors try to collect pollen from flowers?
Does there appear to be any connection between the variety of insect visitors and the shape of flowers?
Do more insects appear at certain times of the day than others?
Are there certain weather conditions that seem to be more suitable for insects?

There is no doubt also that a successful investigation of this type may help children to discover many more problems to tackle. It is always necessary to remember that for the children the thinking involved in designing an investigation is of more value than the answers, since it is possible that further tests will show some of these to be inaccurate.

Pollination and fertilisation

Children can find the story of pollination in many books, but it is more interesting to try to discover at first hand about the ways the parts of flowers are involved.

Insects and pollen

If you have an opportunity to observe bees entering an observation hive, look for baskets on their third pairs of legs filled with pollen of various colours.
Do many other insects visit flowers? Take a large hand magnifier out of doors and look for small beetles inside blackberry and convolvulus flowers. Do they go to places where pollen can easily fall on to them?

In what flowers is it possible to find stores of nectar? Do guidelines on petals really run towards these stores?

Find the nectar pockets on buttercup petals. Could insect visitors collect from these stores without brushing against ripe anthers?

Extracting food from a flower

What about insects that do not enter flowers ?

In July watch a bee visiting one flower after another of the common hemp nettle or clover. Is it searching for pollen or nectar ?

What do red admiral butterflies do when they rest on the inflorescences of stonecrop (*Sedum spectabile*) in early September ?

In early August cabbage white butterflies and honey bees can often be seen visiting the flowers on clumps of lavender at the same time. Try to compare their behaviour.

Do the anthers of grass flowers contain more pollen in relation to the flower size than the anthers of flowers pollinated by insects ?

With the aid of a stereomagnifier compare the size of some anthers of false oat with those of a fairly small insect-pollinated plant such as herb robert or white dead nettle.

What does a high pollen count mean ? (Much pollen in a sample of air.)

Is the pollen count higher when grasses are in flower ? This count is published in daily newspapers so different periods between March and June can be compared.

Pollen and flowers

Place some ripe stamens on a glass slide and gently tease their anthers apart with two needles in order to release some pollen grains. Examine these carefully under the stereomagnifier.

Place a drop of water on some of the grains and gently lower a cover slip over. Examine single pollen grains by transmitted light with a monocular microscope if available. What sort of surfaces would be most suitable to enable these grains to remain lodged between the hairs of insects' bodies while they travel from flower to flower ?

Feel and look at some stigmas. Are they sufficiently rough or sticky for small grains to adhere to their surfaces ? Are there any grooves in which grains of pollen might lodge ?

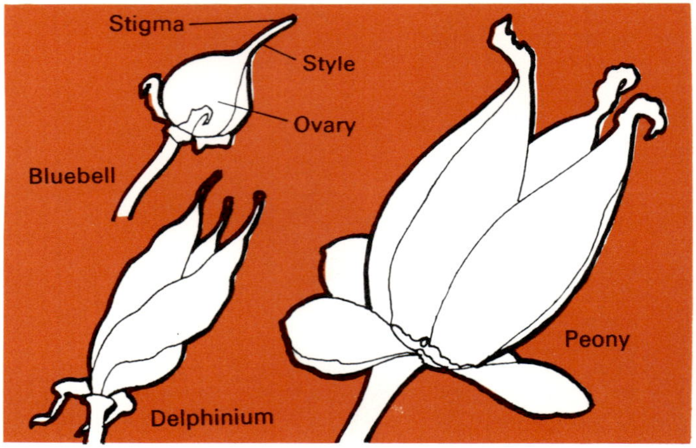

Use a puffer bottle of talcum powder to blow some powder on to the central parts of some large open flowers. Lilies are useful for this test.

Shake the flowers to remove surplus powder and then look at their stigmas under the stereomagnifier. Can any grains of talcum powder be seen adhering to them ?

Examine also the stigmas of older flowers that have been open long enough to have had a chance of becoming pollinated. Can any grains of pollen be found on them ?

What happens when no pollen reaches a stigma ? The flowers of buttercup, dog rose, pea or bean can be used for this investigation.

With fine forceps carefully remove all the stamens from a few flowers as soon as they open. Immediately enclose these flowers in small waterproof Cellophane bags. Compare the central parts of these flowers with those of similar free flowers at the same stage of development two or three weeks after the petals from both sets have withered and fallen. Can you discover any difference?

What could happen to pollen grains that do reach a stigma?

Place some 5% sugar (sucrose) solution in a cavity microscope slide and add some pollen grains to it. Cover with a cover slip and then observe the grains daily with the aid of a microscope. Does anything grow from these grains?

Now find some flowers with large pistils and cut them in halves lengthwise. Bluebells and daffodils are suitable.

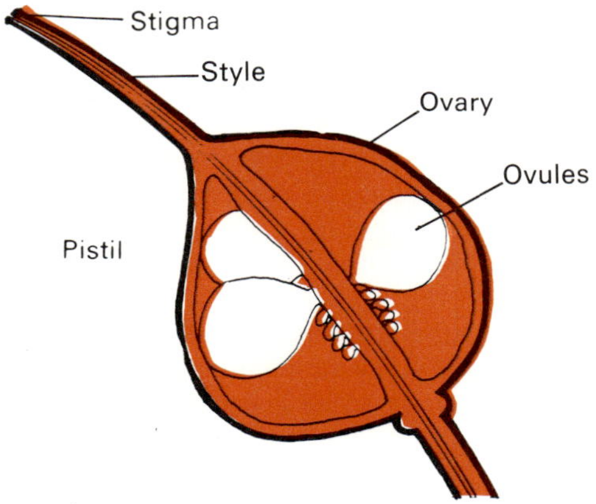

If tubes should grow down the style from pollen grains on the stigma what would they be likely to meet when they penetrate into the ovary?

Children who have been able to make these observations should have no difficulty in accepting the idea that something from pollen grains is likely to meet and join with something in ovules to form seeds. This is the process of fertilisation.

Much later, probably at fifth- or sixth-form stage, the fusion of the pollen and ovular nuclei will be investigated and understanding of what is involved in fertilisation will be greatly extended.

Looking at fruits and seeds

Seeds are fertilised ovules and the ovaries or seed boxes containing them are the fruits.

Single seeds fill some ovaries, and other parts of plants sometimes continue their growth and become closely associated with fruits, as in rose hips. Children may therefore sometimes find difficulty in deciding whether they are examining fruits or seeds. For investigations that are appropriate at this stage this is not likely to matter. Teachers should simply try to increase the children's understanding gradually by using the vocabulary correctly in the course of discussion.

When the petals and stamens of flowers have been shed it is reasonable to assume that fertilisation has taken place.

Then children can look for further developments such as:

The lengthening and swelling of remaining parts.
Changes in colour and texture.
Openings appearing on some fruits.
An increase in the mass of seeds.

Here is some material for observation and comparison:

Peas	Larkspur
Beans	Plantains
Lupins	Canterbury bells
Delphiniums	Hogweed
Poppies	Horse and sweet chestnut

In autumn collect and soak some single-seeded fruits such as acorns, sycamore, maple or sunflower, and some of the large seeds of the horse chestnut, pea and bean. Carefully take them to pieces and look for embryo plants. Which of these plants will be able to draw on good stores of food when they continue their growth?

The dispersal of fruits and seeds

Some plants may be widely distributed because their seeds and fruits are moved about more frequently and over longer distances than those of other species.

Some ways of searching for evidence of travelling fruits and seeds

1. Try to collect material from the air. Here are some devices that can be used for this.

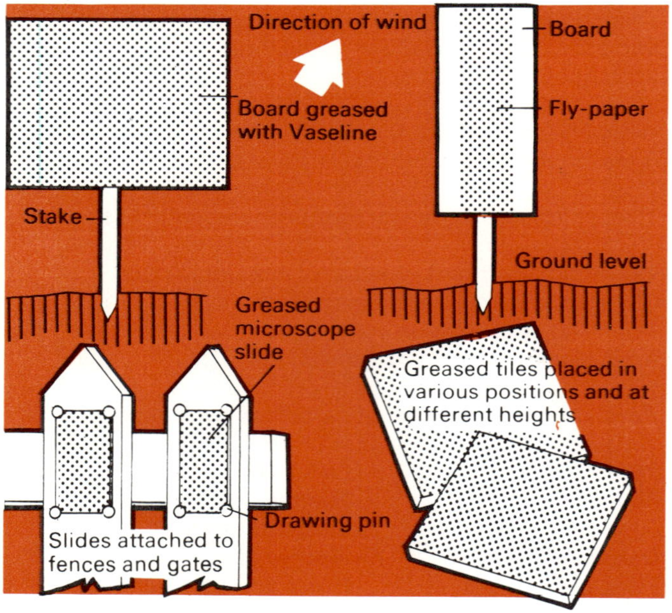

Examine these traps regularly for seeds.

Examine also the spiders' webs on gorse bushes. When rosebay willowherb plants are shedding seeds these may be white with their plumes.

2. Search for plants in places where no human being would sow seeds, for example:

The cracks between paving stones.
The crevices of rocks.
On old walls.
In tree stumps.

3. Examine flower beds. What has become established without the gardener's aid? Fill a seed tray with moist, sterilised potting compost and leave it out of doors. If a plant appears, search for the nearest possible source of seeds, that is, a similar mature plant. How far is it from the tray?

4. Look for a place where sycamore or oak seedlings are abundant and then find the distance between them and the nearest mature trees of the same species. Alternatively begin at a lone sycamore or oak and hunt for seedlings.

5. Collect some of the following:

a. Bird droppings, which you should avoid handling. Pick up with a trowel and place them in a plastic bag.
b. Bird pellets, which must be soaked and teased apart before using.
c. Mud from boots after a country walk.
d. Mud brushed out of a doormat.
e. Mud from the treads of car and tractor tyres.
f. Mud deposited at the side of a meandering stream.

In spring place samples of these materials mixed with moist, sterilised potting compost in separate pots. Cover them with plastic sheeting and examine regularly for the appearance of seedlings.

6 Examine the ground bordering riding tracks on heaths and commons. Do any plants occur frequently there but remain rare or absent in other parts of the area?

7. Examine stockings or trouser legs for hooked fruits after walking through undergrowth or near hedges in late summer or autumn.

8. In woodland look for seeds and fruits that may have been partly eaten by animals and then dropped. Plant them in sterilised compost to find out whether any plants develop. Examine deserted birds' nests for seeds and fruits.

9. Examine your beach-combing collections for fruits and seeds. If you find any, plant them so that you can try to discover whether they have been damaged by a journey in salt water. Can plants grow from seeds of salt marsh plants if given fresh water? What fruits might be transported by ocean currents?

10. Set up some filtering devices in different parts of a shallow flowing stream and regularly examine material in them for seeds or fruits.

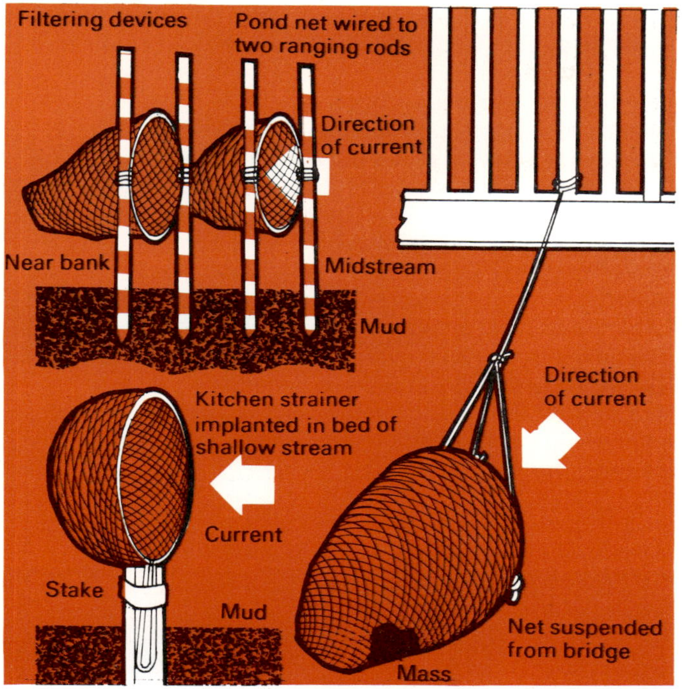

11. Collect some submerged plants from streams and ditches. Float them in a dish of water or sink and examine them for trapped seeds and fruits.

12. Many useful specimens can be obtained from greengrocers' shops. Here children will discover that some things they have known as vegetables, such as marrow, courgettes, beans, peas, are really fruits containing seeds.

At this stage children are unlikely to be interested in much botanical detail and should not be burdened with the names — such as capsule, schizocarp, drupe, etc — relating to different types of fruits.

They will probably use the most obvious similar features as a means of sorting and arranging their collections. These features may arouse their curiosity and encourage them to discover more about the ways in which these parts may aid dispersal.

Times for collecting

It is possible to find some fruits and seeds during any month of the year. Children could make a long-term record of times when various plants in the school grounds and surrounding district are bearing fruit. This record of observations could be as interesting to build up as a record showing when these plants are in flower.

We found our fruits and seeds in these months								
Name of fruit or seed	**April**	**May**	**June**	**July**	**Aug**	**Sept**	**Oct**	**Nov**
Groundsel	■	■	■	■	■	■	■	■
Dandelion		■	■	■	■	■	■	■
Sow-thistle				■	■			
Rosebay willowherb					■	■		
Goat's beard				■	■	■		
Thistle				■	■	■		
Old man's beard						■	■	
Sycamore					■	■		
Maple					■	■		
Ash					■	■	■	
Elm		■	■					
Birch						■	■	
Lime					■	■		
Hornbeam					■	■		
Hogweed				■	■	■	■	
Burdock				■	■	■	■	■
Common avens *(Geum)*					■	■	■	
Cleavers			■	■	■	■		
Lupin			■	■	■	■		
Delphinium				■	■	■		
Poppy					■	■		
Campion				■	■	■		
Balsam					■	■		
Gorse				■	■	■	■	■
Horse chestnut						■	■	
Sweet chestnut						■	■	
Acorn						■	■	
Hip						■	■	
Haw					■	■	■	
Blackberry					■	■		
Plum					■	■		
Apple					■	■	■	
Elderberry				■	■	■	■	

How are fruits and seeds dispersed?

These investigations may help children to think of wind, animals, moving vehicles carrying seeds in the treads of their tyres and water as agents for dispersal. The movement of fruits and seeds reduces the rivalry between a parent plant and seedlings and may help seeds to reach places where there is less competition for space and light.

Are some fruits and seeds moved about more easily than others ? Could any parts of them aid this dispersal ?

A collection of fruits and seeds illustrating the intricacy and variety of the structures attached to them could serve as a good starting point for following up these questions.

Plumed fruits (floaters)

The following have plumed fruits : thistles, dandelions, sow-thistle, groundsel, cat's ear, hawkbit, hawkweed, hawk's-beard, goat's-beard and old man's beard. These will provide plenty of material for children to test.

Fruits of goat's-beard, actual size

The single-seeded fruits of these plants are alike in being extremely light and therefore easily held up above the ground.

Release some of them out of doors on a day when there is a gentle breeze. Try to follow the progress of a single fruit.

In what direction does it travel ?
What is also moving in the same direction ?
Does it rise and sink as it is moved along ?
Does its speed appear to alter ?
About how far does it travel before reaching the ground ?
If it comes to rest on the ground is it raised again and driven onward ? Does this happen many times ?
Are the periods of time spent floating in the air and on the ground similar or uneven ?
Do similar fruits travel in the same way ? Try to time some.
On what does progress seem to depend ?
Are some of these fruits more easily separated from their plumes than others and therefore likely to fall and remain on the ground sooner ?

A dandelion clock magnified to twice its actual size

Warm air rises. Does this suggest that plumed fruits are more likely to be held aloft and driven upwards on hot sunny days and at certain times during the day?

Try keeping a patch of fruiting thistles under observation. Try to estimate whether more thistledown leaves these plants when the weather is:

Sunny and calm.
Sunny and windy.
Dull and calm.
Dull and windy.
Rainy.
Rainy and windy.

All watching periods should be similar in length. The end of August or early September is a good time for doing this.

Compare the movement of some plumed fruits released above a small electric heater or radiator with similar ones set free with no source of heat below them. Could the journeys of plumed fruits be influenced by rising air currents?

Use the stereomagnifier to carefully compare the structure of various plumes. In all cases there are many spaces between the material of which they consist.

A plumed arrangement gives a very large surface area for air currents to push against in relation to the mass of the fruit that has to be supported.

Reducing the surface area of plumes
This can be tested. The plumes of goat's-beard (*Tragopogon pratensis*) are particularly suitable as they are comparatively large.

Begin indoors and use fruits as similar in size as possible.

Prepare the plumes of ten fruits in each of the ways shown in the following diagram.

Then compare the average times taken for each set of fruits to reach the ground when released from a height of 5 m.

Do parts of plumes offer less resistance to the air than whole ones?

What happens to fruits with plumes treated in this way when they are released out of doors in winds of various strengths? Can air currents influence their progress as effectively as when the plumes were whole?

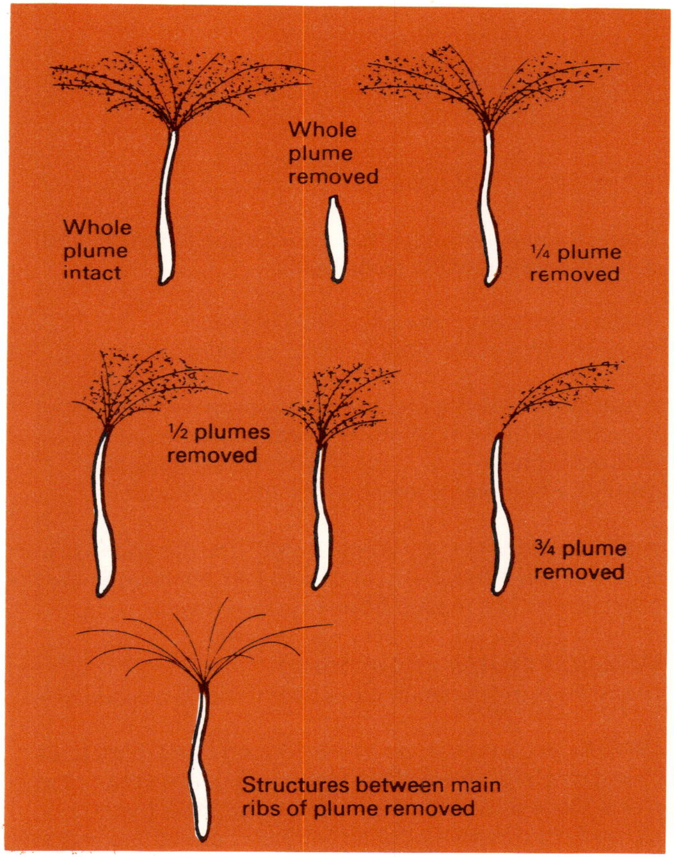

Does moisture affect plumes?
Look at thistledown and feel it after heavy rain. What changes occur as some of it becomes dry?

Plumes attached to goat's-beard or dandelion fruits will become very dry when stored in cardboard boxes. Compare some of them with plumed fruits still adhering to plants after rain or before there has been time for a heavy dew to evaporate.

What angles do the rays of these plumes make with the stalks?

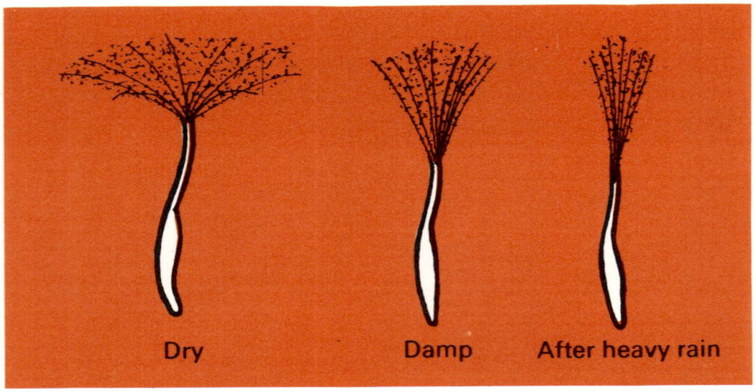

Release some fruits of goat's-beard attached to dry and damp plumes from the same point:

In still air indoors, timing the rates of fall.
In air currents out of doors—try to observe progress.

An air stream can be created by means of a small Moulinex hair dryer. Direct it towards dry and wet plumed fruits lying on a tray of soil representing the ground. Which fruits are raised by the air stream?

Are plumed fruits more likely to reach the ground in dry or wet weather? In what sort of weather conditions are they most likely to be moved from the ground again?

Winged fruits (spinners)

Many fruits produced by trees bear wing-like projections.

With the exception of birch the winged fruits likely to be found by children are much larger and heavier than plumed fruits. Does this mean they cannot be upheld by air currents? Look for evidence beneath trees where winged fruits are ripening.

Try to find out more about the effect of wings by dropping different fruits through still air down the well of a staircase or from a balcony. (Make sure there is no danger of children falling while they do this.)

There are different ways of releasing fruits, therefore in each test make sure that all are treated in the same way.

How many fruits spin as they make the downward journey? About what distances do they travel before spinning begins?

Are winged fruits from the lowest branches of trees likely to spin many times before reaching the ground?
Do the single fruits of sycamore, maple and hornbeam travel differently from pairs?

Does the spinning caused by wings delay the descent of fruits?
Time the journeys of fruits released in the same way, from the same point, with and without wing attachments. Use an average of ten fruits each time.

Better results will be obtained when the distance travelled is more than 10 m.

Children should record their results visually as on this block diagram. In this way they can obtain comparisons of the efficiency of different wings as delaying mechanisms, even though the areas and masses of seeds attached to them vary.

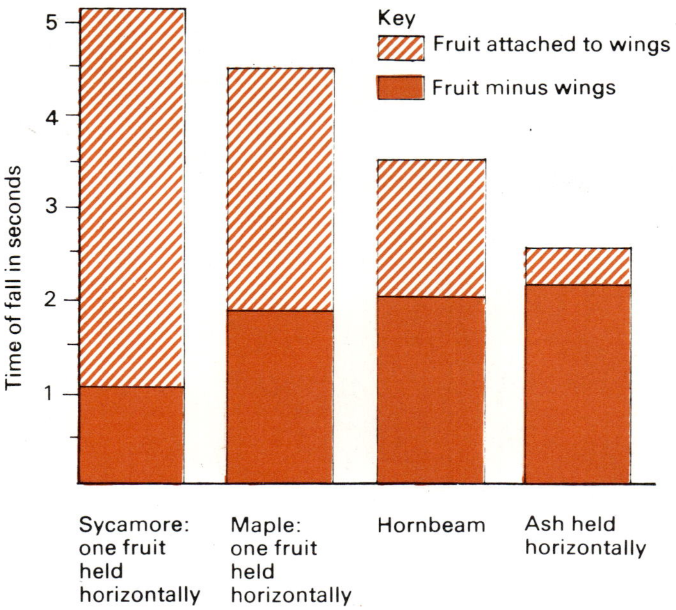

They could express the results of these tests as ratios :

$$\frac{\text{Time of fall with wing}}{\text{Time of fall minus wing}} = \ldots$$

For the sycamore the ratio is $\frac{5{\cdot}2}{1{\cdot}5} = 3{\cdot}7$.

For the maple the ratio is $\frac{4{\cdot}5}{1{\cdot}5} = 3{\cdot}0$.

For the hornbeam the ratio is $\frac{4{\cdot}2}{1{\cdot}6} = 2{\cdot}6$.

For the ash the ratio is $\frac{2{\cdot}6}{1{\cdot}7} = 1{\cdot}5$.

Is any advantage gained if the descent from the parent plant is retarded ?
Begin this investigation indoors by allowing ten sycamore and ten ash fruits to fall downwards through still air. Calculate their average landing positions in relation to a vertical line from the point of release. Now go out of doors and release the same fruits in the same way from the same height. What does the more effective delaying action of the sycamore wings give the air movements time to do ?

Which sycamore fruits are likely to have the best chance of being moved the greatest distance from the parent tree ? Some children may like to take their investigations further by finding out more about the effect of altering the shape of the wings of some fruits.

Hooked fruits (clingers)

Children should be able to collect some fruits of burdock, common avens, cleavers and enchanter's nightshade.

Examine the hooked structures of these specimens with the aid of a stereomagnifier. Do they show much variety ?

The hooks should enable fruits to become attached to animals' coats and people's clothing.

Are they likely to become more firmly attached to certain materials and so be carried for greater distances ?

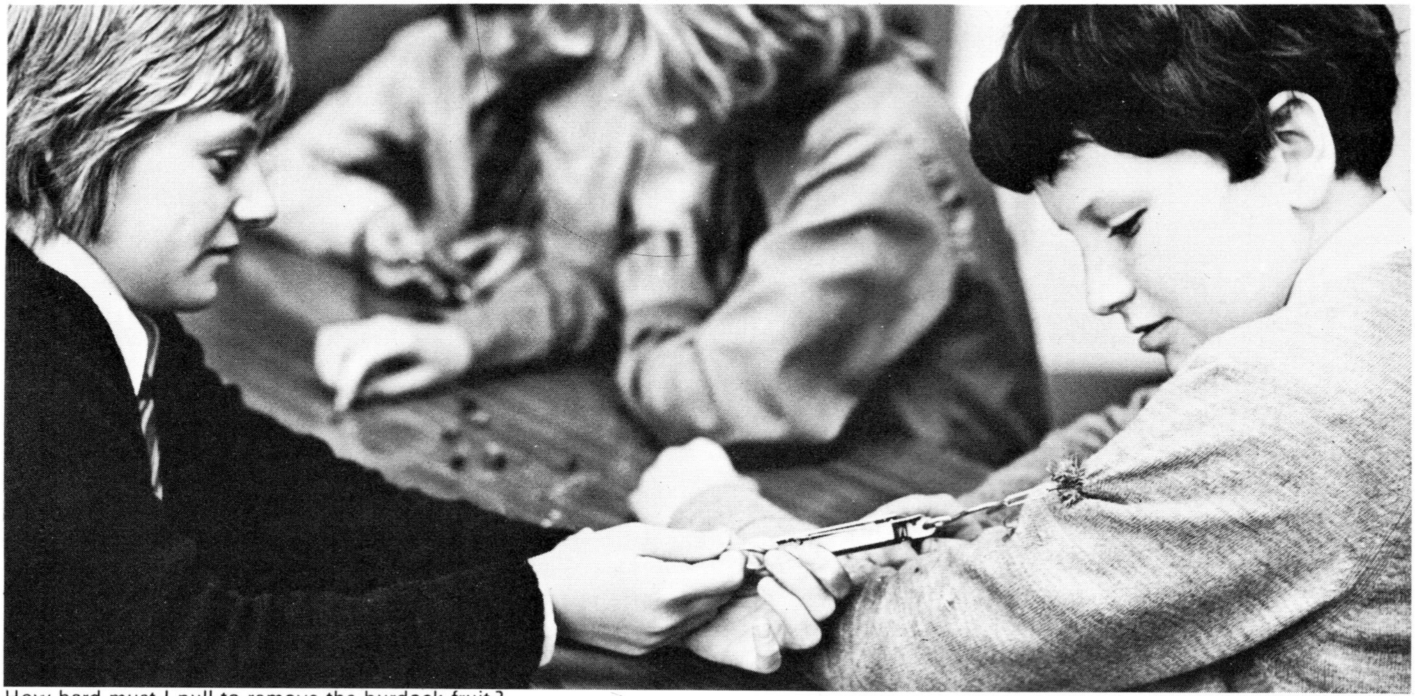
How hard must I pull to remove the burdock fruit?

Testing the clinging power

Use a newton-meter or rubber band to measure the force required to pull fruits from materials. Pass a fisherman's hook attached to a paper clip through the fruit. Hook the newton-meter on to the paper clip.

Materials for testing

Woollen sock
Nylon stocking
Tweed (man's jacket)
Cotton, Nylon, Crimplene (dress materials)
Plastic sheeting
Oilskin (mackintoshes)
Rubber (Wellington boots)
Leather, Canvas (boots and shoes)
Fur, Sheep's wool, Feathers (animal body coverings)

Do the results of the tests support the suggestions that:

Hooked fruits are likely to be carried by mammals rather than birds?
Hooked fruits are less likely to adhere to human clothing on wet days?

Swaying fruits (censers)

In late summer and autumn certain large fruits remain attached to their flower stalks.

The poppy is a good example.

A garden poppy and its fruit

In July cut open some poppy fruits and examine their contents. How can you describe the size and quantity of the seeds they contain?

Are the seeds in other fruits that remain attached to parent plants also small and numerous?

Examine the fruits of campion, love-in-a-mist, Canterbury bell and antirrhinum.

Fruit of love-in-a-mist

Now examine some newly formed poppy fruits which are still at the stage of being green and tender. Is it possible to find any way of escape for the seeds inside?

What appears on the walls of these fruits as they dry and harden?

Place some dry poppy fruits on which the openings are visible in water. Is it still possible to see these openings after the fruits have been soaked for a time?

Now examine some campion fruits in both wet and dry states.

Seeds escape through openings in these fruits as they sway to and fro in the wind. Is this more likely to happen in dry or wet weather?

Children can have some fun and find many opportunities for discussing the problems involved in the escape of seeds from swaying fruits when they try to assess the effect of introducing variables into their otherwise similar home-made models of these fruits.

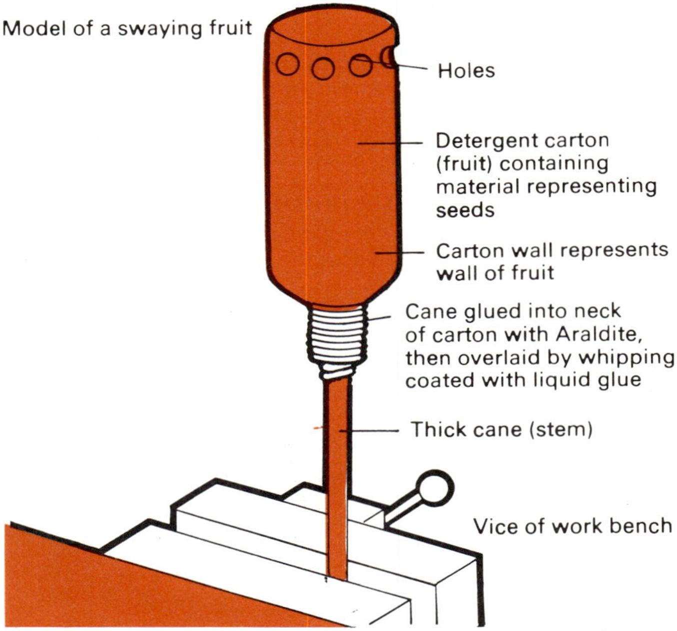

Tapioca, lentils, mustard seeds or the smallest expanded polystyrene balls can be placed in the detergent carton to serve as seeds. Avoid sand which might get into children's eyes and cause damage.

Cause the model to sway by gently pulling the carton and releasing it. Escaping seeds can be collected from the floor or a sheet placed beneath the model. The quantity can be found by counting or weighing.

Here are some variables that children can introduce:

The number of seeds in relation to the size of fruit.
The type, size and mass of the seeds.
The size, number and distance apart of the holes.
The arrangement of the holes — regular or haphazard.
The position of the holes — high or low — on the carton.
The length and the dryness or wetness of the stems.
The size and number of swings made by the model fruit.

A long-term investigation

This can be undertaken if there is suitable space in the school grounds.

Plant one poppy seedling. In August leave the fruits on this plant.

Plot the positions of poppy plants in relation to the parent during the following summer (June). If these plants can be allowed to develop, continue to plot the positions of new seedlings.

Splitting fruits (projectiles)

As some fruits develop, they split, shooting out their contents with some force. Could this be due to contraction caused by loss of water?

Laburnum pods splitting. Seeds are poisonous to children

Collect some well-developed broom or lupin pods and weigh them. Continue recording their mass daily. Compare the mass of this material when the pods have split open with the first weighing. Has there been any loss?

If you are near some gorse bushes on a hot summer day, listen for the popping of fruits as they split and project their seeds.

Touch-me-not (*Impatiens noli-tangere*), one of the balsam family, is not common, but some might be grown from seed in a shady damp place. In this way children can find out how far the seeds scatter when they make the ripe fruits explode by lightly touching their tips. Perhaps the person who named this plant also did this.

The curled-up empty seed cases of pansy, vetch, hop trefoil and black medick could also be collected. Can the cases be uncurled by soaking them in water?

These experiences may arouse children's interest in catapults and other projecting devices. Perhaps they could make and use some models to find out more about the relationship between the path followed by a projected body and the force with which it is pushed. This sort of investigation must have been carried out when siege engines attacked castle and city walls in the Middle Ages.

Fleshy fruits

The attractively coloured juicy parts of these fruits are attractive to man and many animals.

Offer a choice to birds to see whether it is possible to discover the ones collected most frequently. Attach fruits in positions corresponding to those they occupy on bushes.

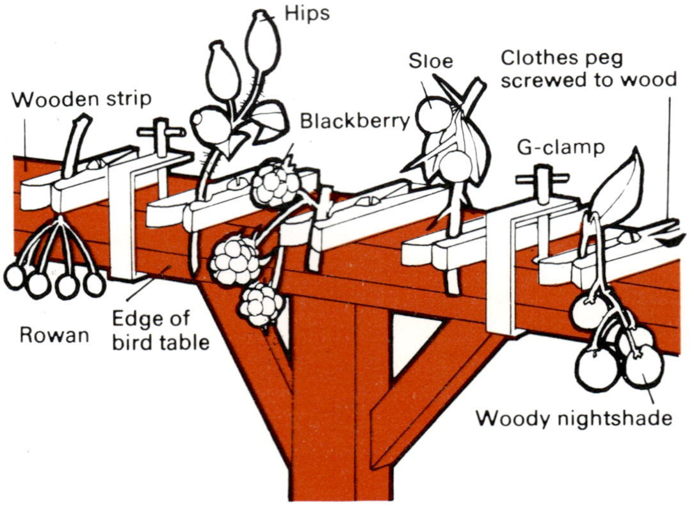

It is thought that the seeds of these fruits germinate after passing through birds' bodies. If so they are resistant to digestive juices. How easily can seeds be harmed?

Collect some seeds of these fleshy fruits. Soak them in hydrochloric acid of varying strengths (10%, 20%, 30%), and then plant them in potting compost. Record the number germinating.

Tomato plants often grow from seeds that collect at sewage farms. Obviously they have not been affected by human digestive juices.

What happens to plum and date stones, apple, pear, grape, orange and grapefruit pips, and the stones from avocado pears ? Children can try to collect information.

What results are obtained when one tries to grow plants from material of this sort ? Can germination be speeded up by damaging the hard coverings of seeds such as dates ?

Is this the easiest way of producing new plants ? What methods do fruit growers employ ?

Hard fruits

Children will find no special structures likely to aid the dispersal of acorns, beech and hazel nuts, sweet chestnut and horse chestnut fruits. They may be carried to the food stores of woodland animals such as squirrels. Children move many acorns and horse chestnut seeds. Will these hard fruits float if they reach rivers ? What is the density of a conker or acorn compared to that of water ? Do officers of the Forestry Commission collect and store tree seeds ?

5 Discovering relationships between form and function in animals

Parts of dead animals found in the countryside can be very useful specimens to examine for possible relationships between form and function. It is always necessary to remember that these things may carry bacteria of diseases that can be transmitted to human beings. Therefore any of this material that is brought into school should be treated with disinfectant. Rubber gloves should be used for handling. Teachers should make sure that children are fully aware of the possible dangers and that they wash their hands thoroughly in water containing disinfectant if they touch dead animal material. This is good health education.

Insect legs

Children observing living insects may make suggestions about the ways in which parts of their bodies, particularly their legs, are used. These ideas can be tested by careful examination of specimens that can be magnified easily.

Preparing a collection

Some teachers may like to use the resources at a teachers' centre for preparing a collection of slides of insects' legs to add to the school resources.

Carefully remove the legs from the bodies of dead insects with a fine pair of forceps. Boil in 10% sodium hydroxide solution for 10 minutes. This should detach the soft tissue from the chitinous exoskeleton of the legs. Any remaining tissue should be teased off with a dissecting needle.

Wash the specimens in running water for 2–3 minutes to remove the sodium hydroxide. Remove all water from the legs by passing them through solutions containing the following percentages of alcohol : 30%, 50%, 70%, 90%. The specimens should remain in each solution for 2 minutes. Finally they should be steeped in absolute alcohol for the same amount of time.

This treatment in stages ensures that the chitinous material of the legs is not damaged by drastic changes.

Transfer the specimens to Xylene to make them transparent.

To mount a specimen place a small drop of Canada balsam on a microscope slide. Use forceps to transfer the specimen to the drop. Then use a dissecting needle to lower a cover slip gently over this, taking care to see that no air bubbles become trapped beneath the cover slip. Leave undisturbed for a few days to allow the Canada balsam to harden.

Suggestions for a collection

Terrestrial insects

1. Cockroach, locust.

These insects have walking and running legs.

A cockroach feeding on bread

2. Honey bee.

The first pair each bears a comb for cleaning antennae.
The second pair each bears a prong for digging pollen out of the baskets on the third pair of legs.
The third pair bears on each an arrangement of stiff bristles forming the pollen basket as well as bristles serving as brushes.

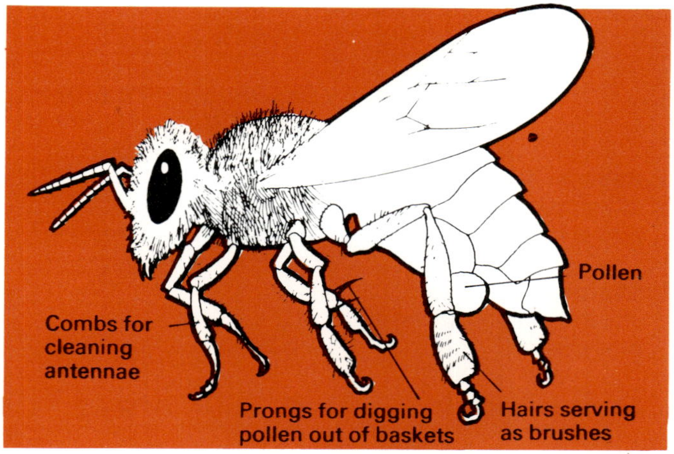

3. House fly or bluebottle.

The ends of the legs bear suckers to enable the fly to walk on walls and ceilings.

4. Crane fly (daddy-long-legs).

This has very long and slender legs.

5. Beetle.

This is a good example of walking legs.

6. Caterpillar of cabbage white butterfly.

This insect has two types of legs. The front three pairs, known as the true insect legs, are for walking, while its pairs of stumpy cushion legs enable it to cling to surfaces.

7. Cabbage white butterfly.

The legs should be compared with the true insect legs of its larval stage.

Aquatic insects

1. Water scorpion.

The first pair of legs is modified for seizing food.

A water scorpion using its front pair of legs to capture food

2. Water boatman.

The third pair of legs is modified for rowing.

3. Male carnivorous water beetle.

The first pair has discs bearing suckers for clinging to the female during mating.
The third pair is modified for rowing.

When children have had opportunities of examining a considerable number of insect legs, they can begin to consider whether there is a general pattern for these structures among insects. Can individual differences be related to the way the legs are used?

Collections of other useful parts

Teachers interested in laboratory techniques may like to prepare more collections of specimens for the children's use. Here are some suggestions.

1. The mouth parts of insects. They should be prepared by the same method as described above for legs. Such a collection can be studied in relation to food capture and dealing with what is caught.

2. Birds' beaks. Useful for relating to feeding habits.

3. Birds' skulls. For preparation, see Volume 4, page 69. These will also be useful in discussions about feeding habits.

4. Birds' feet. No special preparation is required other than washing in water containing some disinfectant. This collection will be suitable when considering the movement and feeding behaviour of birds.

5. Mammals' teeth. No special preparation is required for this collection. It will be useful when considering feeding habits.

6. Birds' feathers. See Volume 2 Part 2, page 94. These are useful when considering adaptations for flight.

Size and shape

The size and shape of some animals' bodies or certain of their organs can be related to their habits. Many good suggestions for discovering more about this topic are given in the Nuffield O-level Biology Course Books. See the table below for references.

	Student's Text II	***Teacher's Guide II***
Relationship between size of animals and supporting power of their limbs	pp. 56–67	pp. 49–57
The influence of streamlining on speed of movement	pp. 69–71	pp. 58
Shape and support	pp. 72–78	pp. 58–59
Surface area and its relationship to heat loss or conservation	pp. 82–89	pp. 61–66
Surface area and loss or conservation of water	pp. 89–93	pp. 66–69

A burrowing animal

In country districts children may be able to observe living moles and examine dead specimens. Gamekeepers and mole catchers can be helpful in providing material.

The mole lives underground and moves through the soil in search of food. Plot the distribution of mole hills week by week in a field or lawn infested by moles. How frequently do changes occur?

If you can get a live one, place it on soft earth and note the time it takes to disappear.

A mole emerging from the soil

See *School Projects in Natural History*, no. 1, pages 7 and 14 for further suggestions for fieldwork on the digging activities of moles. This book can be obtained from the Devon Trust for Nature Conservation, Slapton Ley Field Centre, Kingsbridge, Devonshire.

If a preserved specimen is available, examine :

1. The size of the eyes. Do animals that live in darkness need eyes ?

2. The length of snout. In what way would a mole find a good sense of smell useful ?

3. The shape of the body ; the directions in which the fur can be stroked. Could these characteristics enable the mole to slip through the soil easily ?

4. The width of the hand on the forelimb. Could this serve as a spade ?

5. The length and size of the hind limbs. Are they of a suitable size for avoiding getting in the way as the animal digs with its forelimbs ?

6. Try using spades as levers for moving some dry sand or soil in the same way as a mole is known to use its forelimbs for burrowing.

Which is the better tool for this :

A spade with a large or small blade ?
A spade with a long or a short handle ?

Is there any similarity between a mole's forelimb and the type of spade chosen ?

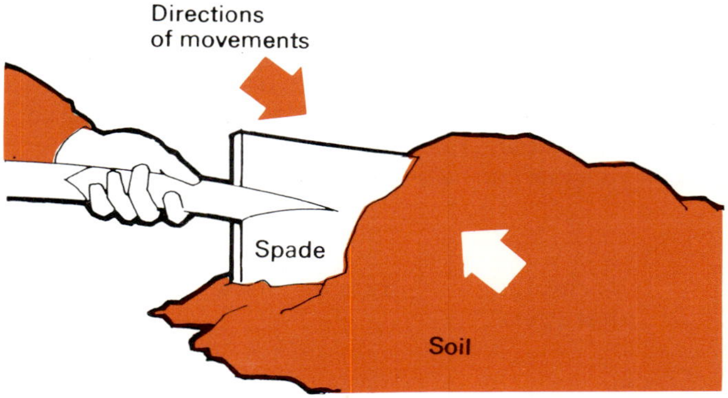

Conclusion
Every time that children try to discover more about the ways the organs of living things work, their teachers can encourage them to ask questions, for example :

Is this a good arrangement ?
Is this way of achieving the result better than any others we have found so far ?
To what extent can close relationships between form and function be found in living animals ?

6 Variation and adaptation

Again and again as children sort and arrange their various collections, they will group together certain living things on the basis of likeness, but as they do this do they also become interested in the fact that the things within any such set are also different. Only man-made objects, for example coins of the same value or mass-produced factory-made commodities, can be identical.

The individuality of living things has great significance. Many investigations through which deeper understanding of this concept of *variation* can be gained are still beyond children of thirteen. However, it is not too soon for some experience that can help them to begin thinking.

What characters can vary?

The first step might be a search for collections of living things that vary within their common patterns, and the mounting of a classroom display of these discoveries. This will become an absorbing group project and provide much material for further investigation and discussion.

At this stage it does not matter whether children find their examples within closely defined groups such as single species or from larger sets divisible into sub-sets.
Here are some suggestions for activities.

Variable character	Sets for observation	Individual things showing variation	Method of recording discoveries
Colour	Trees	Autumn leaves	Preserved specimens
		On the same day in October collect 100 leaves and sort according to the colour occupying the largest area on each leaf.	Paintings Coloured photographs
		Examine leaves from: Same tree. Different trees.	Bar graphs
		Leaves should be taken from trees not ground.	
	Cabbage white butterflies	Chrysalids found in different places	Specimens (one of each type)
	Butterflies and moths (Lepidoptera)	Chrysalids	
	Snails	Shells	Specimens

Variable character	Sets for observation	Individual things showing variation	Method of recording discoveries
Colour	Mice in pet shops	Coats	Written record, drawings
	Cats or dogs owned by children in the year group	Coats	Bar graphs
	Pigeons in Trafalgar Square or kept as pets	Feathers	Bar graphs
	Children in the class or year group	Hair Eyes	Mounted clippings from the children Bar graphs
Shape	Trees and shrubs	Leaves	Preserved specimens
	Flowers	Petals	
	Ivy plants in the school grounds	Leaves	
	Trees	Outlines	Silhouettes
	Birds	Wings Beaks	Silhouettes, drawings or specimens
	Insects	Mouth parts	Slides made by the teacher for viewing by stereomicroscope
	Seashore molluscs	Shells	Drawings, specimens
Pattern 	Herd of Friesian cows	Black and white areas of the body	Drawings or photographs
	Clover plants Cuckoo pint plants	Markings on leaves	Preserved specimens or diagrams
	Variegated privet	Green and yellow areas of leaves	
Flavour	Apples	The same children should taste all specimens and then try to reach agreement about this experience.	Written account

Variable character	Sets for observation	Individual things showing variation	Method of recording discoveries
Size	All boys or girls in year group between ages of $12\frac{1}{2}$ years and $12\frac{3}{4}$ years	Heights Mass Hand spans Lengths of middle fingers Shoe sizes	Bar graphs
Size of sunflower seeds 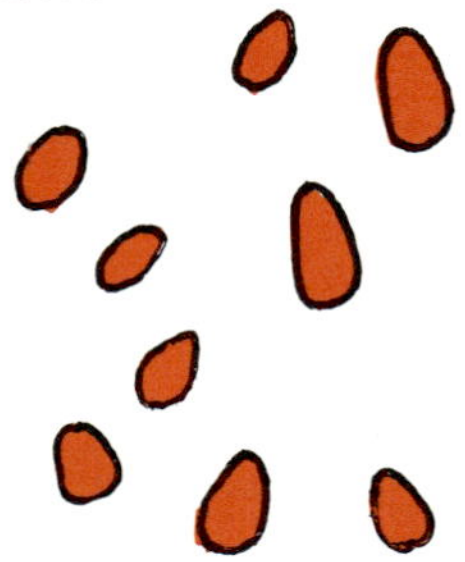	Broad bean seeds from the same packet	Lengths and/or widths — measure with calipers	
	All sunflower fruits from the same plant	Lengths — measure with calipers	
	Acorns from the same tree	Girth, assessed by a grading device	
	Leaves from the same shrub	Lengths of 100 specimens	
Number	Lesser celandine (*Ranunculus ficaria*) Common camomile (*Chamaemelum nobile*)	Petals	Bar graphs
Lupin pods 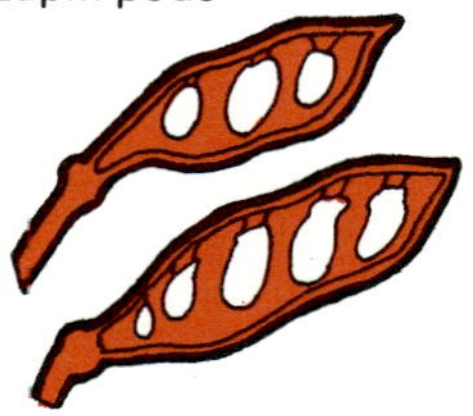	Lupin fruits Delphinium fruits	Seeds contained by fruits	
	Fruits from lime trees	Number of fruits attached to wings	
	Cockle shells	Ribs	
Time	Trees	Leaf fall Note dates of: First colour changes. First falls to ground. Different fraction of tree still bearing leaves. When trees are bare. Records extending over several years and associated with weather records are particularly valuable.	Chart showing dates and estimations

Variable character	Sets for observation	Individual things showing variation	Method of recording discoveries
Time Tadpoles 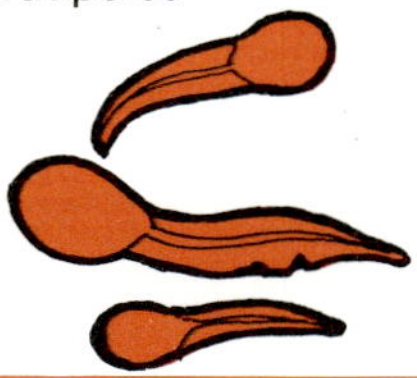	Caterpillars of cabbage white butterfly kept under same conditions Tadpoles from same mass of frog spawn Seeds from same packet	Rate of growth Life histories Germination and growth rates	Curves on same graph Chart with dates, comments and diagrams Graphs
Perception by means of human sense organs	All members of class	Hearing: Compare distances at which ticking watch can be heard. Sight: Compare distances at which a row of printed capital letters can be read accurately.	Bar graphs
Athletic performance	All children in class	Time taken to run or swim 100 m Height or length achieved in jumping (Are best performances achieved by the tallest children?)	Bar graphs
Handwriting	Adults	Signatures (style of handwriting)	Mounted specimens
Ability to profit by experience	Laboratory white rats Children in same year group	Decrease in time taken to find a route through a maze Marks obtained in tests Note. These should be obtained from another class or school by the teacher. In this way unfortunate comparisons between members of the class doing this work can be avoided.	Curves on same graph Bar graphs
Human attitudes	All children in the year group	Favourite colour Favourite TV programme Favourite type of story	Bar graphs

While this work is in progress the children could also be encouraged to read about some great naturalists' observations of variation.

What dates did Gilbert White * mention frequently in his letters? (The departure and appearance of migratory birds.)

When Charles Darwin † was journeying round the world on the survey ship HMS *Beagle,* what did he discover on the Galapagos Islands that gave him so much food for thought? (Variation in the beaks of finches.)

How did Konrad Lorenz ‡ distinguish between the water shrews he kept for a time? (By the markings on the bodies.)

The first discovery that might arise out of discussing this work is the great number of characters of living things that can vary.

Are there any characters that remain always in the same state?

How do characters vary?

Do all characters vary in the same way?

If this question is asked at a time when children can examine many examples of variation, they will probably find some features that are distinctly different in individuals, such as eye colour or markings on clover leaves. They will also find others that vary gradually and are seen, therefore, as larger or smaller versions of the same thing, like rats' tails of different lengths, or greater or lesser numbers of ribs on cockle shells. The characters that can increase or decrease gradually in this latter way are said to vary *continuously*.

* *White, G.,* The Natural History of Selborne *(published by White's brother Benjamin in 1788).*
†*Darwin, C.,* The Voyage of the Beagle, *chapter 17 (John Murray, 1890).*
‡*Lorenz, K.,* King Solomon's Ring, *chapter 9 (Methuen, 1952).*

Distribution of a variation

If a character like a hand-span can have different sizes we might ask: what size do most people have? The best way of finding out is to measure the size in as many people of the same age as possible.

This type of investigation will involve the collection of much data. If the data are arranged in an ordered rather than a haphazard way, possibly on a graph, there will be more chance of any pattern in the distribution of different lengths becoming clear.

The teacher's role in helping children to sort and arrange the results of their observations is, therefore, most important.

Here are some examples of studies that did reveal a pattern. Work like this could be tackled by children in many places.

A group of rather slow-learning children in a large urban school near Rochester often searched some rough ground near their school field for interesting material. One year in late July the pods of the tufted vetch (*Vicia cracca*) were conspicuous and several children became interested in the number of seeds they contained.

When their first counts revealed variation the teacher encouraged them to continue with the investigation and soon everybody in the class was opening pods and recording the numbers of seeds found.

Later the teacher helped the children to find a systematic way of setting out all this information by encouraging them to imagine piles of their pods arranged in order according to the number of seeds they contained.

Graph made with piles of vetch pods

Then on a graph these piles were represented by vertical bars.

How many seeds in pods of tufted vetch ?

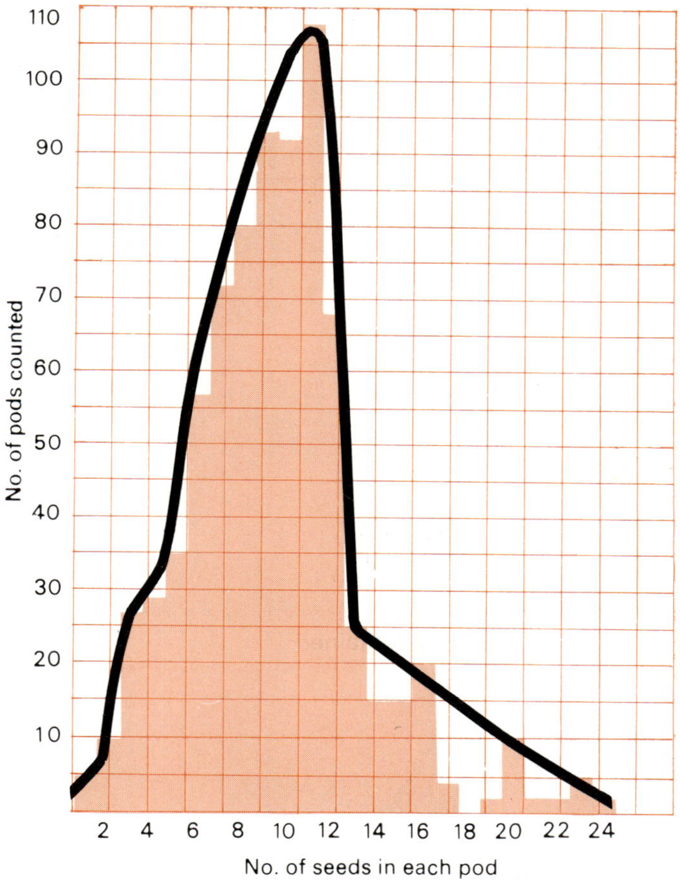

This type of graph, which shows, for example, the number of times or *frequency* with which each quantity of seeds in a pod can be counted is known as a *frequency distribution* or *histogram*, but there is no need to burden the children with such names at present.

Another group of thirteen-year old children became concerned with the way in which the lengths of leaves on the school privet hedge varied. The hundred twigs they collected from this hedge provided many leaves, so these children found it convenient to condense the width of their graph by recording the number of measurements falling within 5-mm intervals.

How is the variation in length of privet leaves distributed?

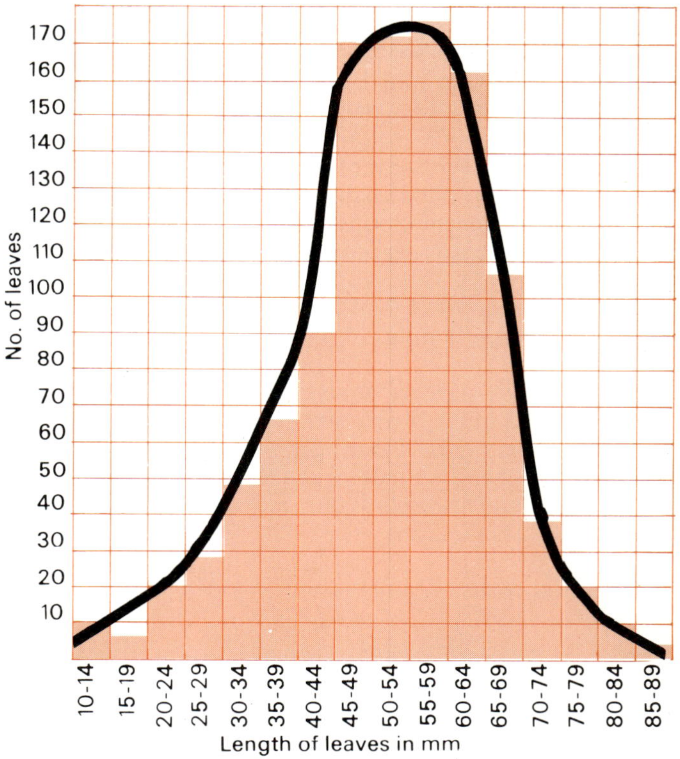

Both these histograms have similar outlines like the well-known *normal curve*, that is, the numbers of seeds in vetch pods and the lengths of privet leaves are distributed *normally* among the total number counted (the *population*).

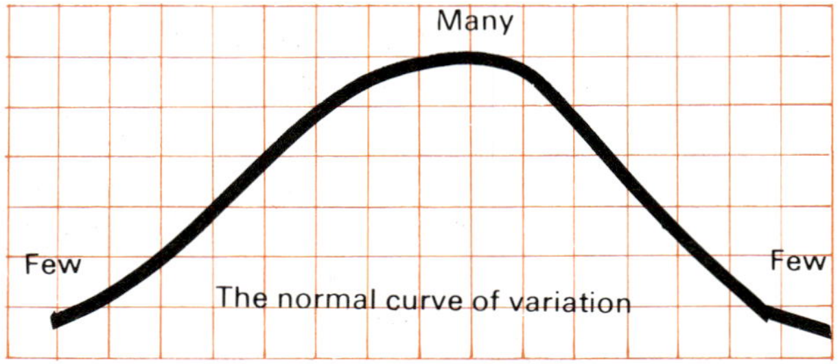

'Normally', in this context, means that *many* of the items are of medium size, but that there are gradual reductions in number as the character under investigation becomes larger or smaller.

Sampling

The numbers of all the vetch pods on the waste ground and all the privet leaves in the hedgerow were too many for the children to examine, so they dealt with randomly selected samples. They were able to discover the normal pattern of distribution in each case because their samples were sufficiently large (797 vetch pods and 1,131 leaves) to be adequately representative of all the pods on the site or all the privet leaves on the bush. (See Volume 3 Part 2, page 20.) For these investigations large classes to deal with the measuring and counting proved distinctly advantageous.

Children can convince themselves of the necessity of a sufficiently large sample.

Collect 100 acorn seeds fallen from the same tree. Group these in 5 sets of 20. Measure the lengths of fruits in one set and draw a histogram showing the results. Is the outline of this anything like a normal curve? Repeat with the second, third, fourth and fifth sets in turn, and each time add the results to the histogram.

Compare successive outlines with the ideal normal curve.

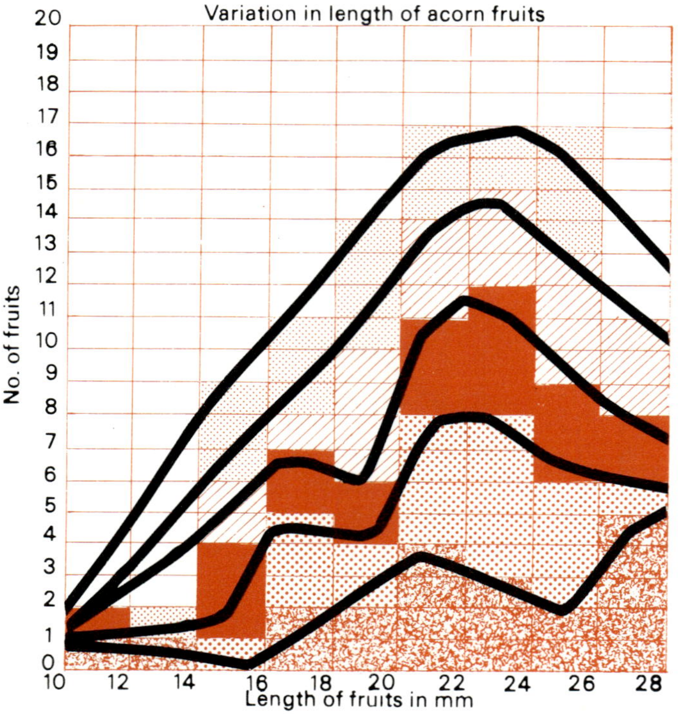

As children grasp the idea of a normal distribution they often become very interested in collecting more examples of variations distributed in this way and cheerfully share out the necessary labour of counting or measuring involved.

Sometimes they may find the results they obtain puzzling. Here, for example, is a histogram representing the different numbers of fruits attached to a sample of 912 wings from a branch of a lime tree blown down by a mid-August gale.

Variation in the number of lime fruits attached to wings
7 August 1973

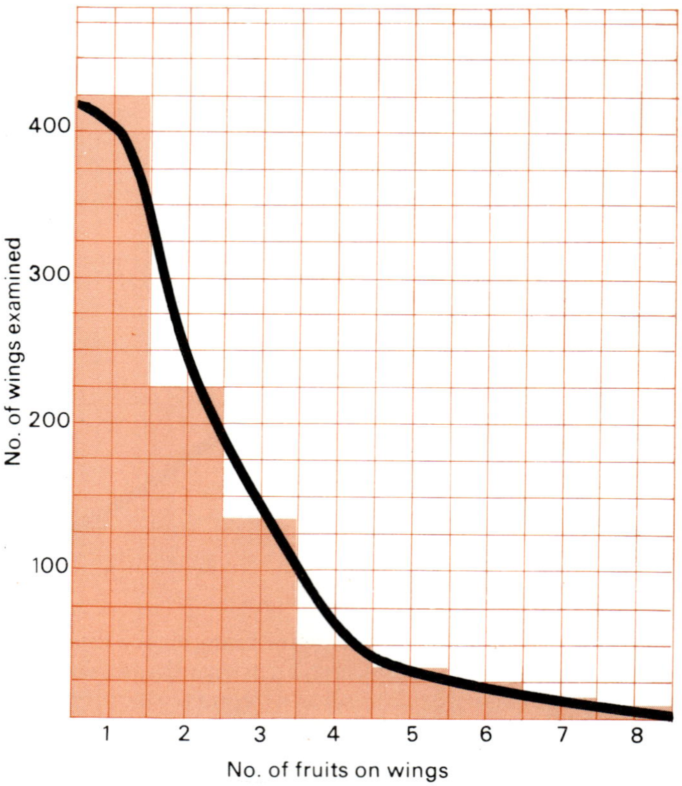

Further counts of material of the same sort gave similar results. Here we have half of a normal curve. It indicates that the variation in an increasing number of fruits per wing is normally distributed. However, the pattern of distribution in the opposite direction cannot be shown because it is impossible to have fractions or negative numbers of fruits attached to lime wings.

Environmental conditions and variation

Plantains are good plants for this investigation because they can be found in many places and their leaves often vary widely in size.

Samples from places where environmental conditions are distinctly different are needed.

Collect a sample from a study area by selecting a few plants at random in similar stages of development. Compare the state of the flowers or fruits in order to decide on the stage they are at.

Remove all the leaves except the very immature ones in the centre of each rosette.

Continue until the whole sample consists of at least 100 leaves.

Here are two studies that children could tackle.

A study of leaves from ratstail plantain (*Plantago major*)

These leaves can easily be distinguished from those of the hoary plantain or lamb's tongue (*Plantago media*) by the abrupt change in width between their leaf blades and leaf stalks, and the length of the leaf stalks.

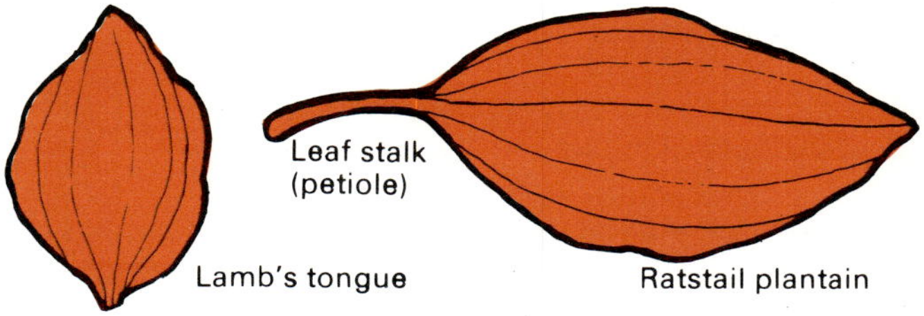

Two samples, each of 100 leaves, were collected from:

A shady sheltered situation.
The open grassland of a recreation ground, frequently mown and trampled.

The broadest part of each leaf in each sample was measured and the results recorded on histograms.

Variation in the leaves of ratstail plantain (*Plantago major*)

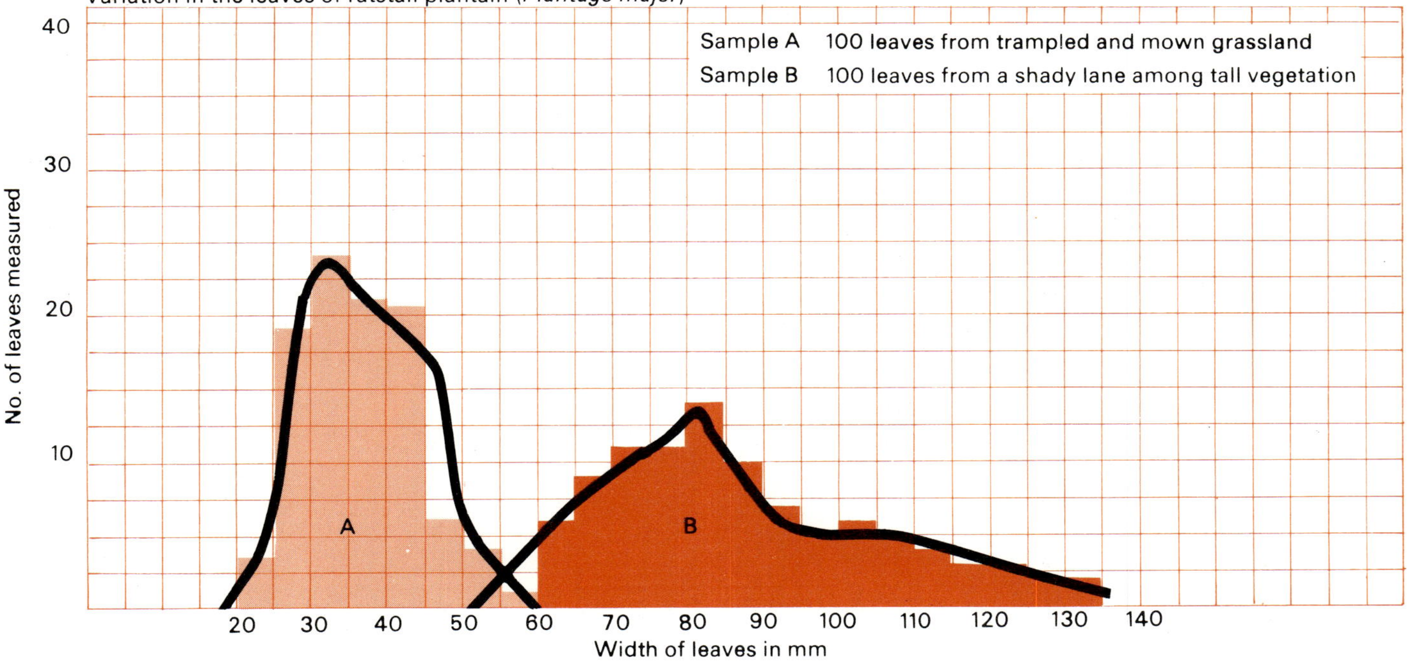

A study of leaves from ribwort plantain (*Plantago lanceolata*)

In this comparison each sample consisted of 200 leaves this time, from plants from :

Waste ground exposed to wind, sunlight and trampling. Woodland where they were shaded and sheltered by many tall trees and plants.

The length of a leaf was taken as the distance from the base of its leaf stalk to its apex.

This distance was measured for each leaf of each sample and the data was then used in constructing a second pair of histograms.

Children could now make some comparison of the two sets of measurements of the plantain leaves by looking carefully at the histograms representing them.

At a considerably later stage they may learn how to use certain mathematical techniques for making valid comparisons of samples consisting of different numbers of specimens. Here the samples compared are of equal size.

What might children say about these graphs ? Possibly that :

Leaves in the exposed places tend to be smaller than those shaded by taller plants and that there is less difference between the largest and smallest leaves than in the other sample.

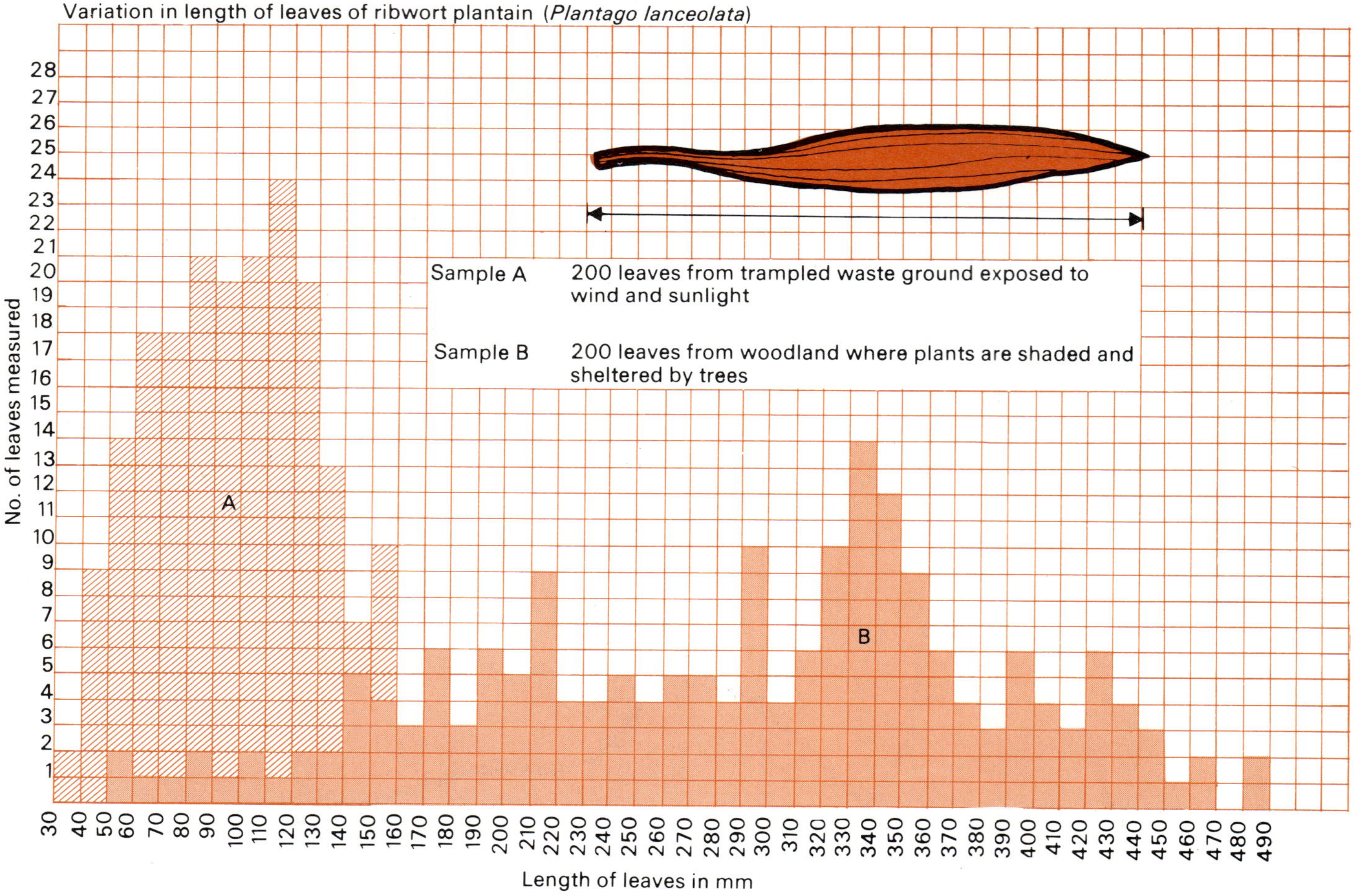

Other comparisons

Here are some other things that children might try comparing.

Samples	Differences in environmental conditions	Character for measurement
Brussels sprouts buds from two plants grown from seed from same packet	End or centre of same row or plot Permeable (sand) or impermeable (clay) soil	Length of each bud cut lengthwise to give a smooth surface for measurement
Plants of woody nightshade (*Solanum dulcamara*)	Exposed shingle beach (as at Dungeness) In shade cast by a hedgerow Competing with other tall plants	Height of each plant in its natural position
Acorns from 2 oak trees of same species	Solitary position or in dense woodland	Girth or length of each fruit

Avoid complications by seeing that children compare samples of equal size collected at the same time.

Will living things reared under similar conditions be alike?

If the type of experience described in the above section gives children evidence of differences in environmental conditions increasing the variation of certain characters, they may easily be interested in the contrary idea: whether living things reared in similar conditions will be alike.

Children could begin tackling this question with some fieldwork in the local supermarket.

Look carefully at the cartons of mustard or cress plants sold for salads. These plants appear to have been grown under very similar conditions. Does careful measurement of leaves or stems reveal any variation? If so, can this be related to any environmental differences?

Now try growing sets of plants from the same type of seeds under similar and different environmental conditions.

Choose rapidly germinating seeds such as mustard, cress, radish, wheat or sunflower from the same packet or plant. Make careful measurements of the plants produced.

Between which sets is the smallest amount of variation found?

If seed can be collected from plantain plants of the same species but varying with regard to leaf size, it can also be used for trials.

Make some measurements of leaves from both types of parent plants. Keep the two sets of seeds apart but give them all similar conditions for growth.

Is there more or less variation in the leaves of plants produced under these conditions than between the leaves of their parents?

If seeds from large-leaved and small-leaved plantain plants, grown under similar conditions, do develop into plants bearing leaves approximately similar in size, we have evidence of another important fact.

When differences in environmental conditions cause a character such as leaf size to vary, such a variation is not permanent. It may or may not appear in plants of the next generation.

How could this apply to plantain plants?

The range of size within which leaves of these plants can vary is wide, but it has limits. Whatever the environmental conditions, plantain leaves never become as big as the largest rhubarb leaves or as small as those of duckweed.

In each generation of plantain plants the size that leaves reach within their range is what is influenced by environmental conditions. While the conditions remain unchanged, leaves of succeeding generations of plants will remain approximately similar in size, but when seeds of the new generation develop under different conditions their leaf size may reach a different position on the range.

Genetic variation

What is interesting about this collection of dandelion leaves?

Sets *B* and *C* came from two plants equally shaded by a hedge, growing 40 mm apart on a neglected lawn.

Set *A* came from a plant on a grassed strip constantly exposed to mowing and trampling, which drained a concrete drive.

Again it seems that differences in environmental conditions have had some influence on the size of all these leaves.

In what way do leaves from sets *A* and *B* show more similarity to each other than to leaves of set *C*? (The shape and number of leaf serrations.)

Have we found a character here that is not varying in response to environmental conditions?

A study of the same characters in plants of different generations might shed more light on this problem.

Collect four or five dandelion plants with leaves whose deep serrations are distinctly different in size and number. When digging up the plants take care to obtain a good length of the main tap root.

Number each plant and record measurements of the size of its leaves and details concerning their serrations.

Now use a vegetative method to produce two new plants from each of the original specimens.

Split the upper 5–10 cm of the roots of these plants lengthwise into two pieces of equal sizes. Plant them separately in John Innes no. 1 compost in 15-cm pots.

Label each pot with the number of the parent plant. Water regularly and keep all pots in the same environmental conditions for 8–10 weeks.

Compare all the second-generation plants. Which character in plants of the new generation now varies less than in the previous generation?

Which character still varies very distinctly and therefore does not appear to have been affected by the uniform environmental conditions?

Sir Edward Salisbury* mentions another common plant that repays careful study—the Oxford ragwort (*Senecio squalidus*). Children using derelict land in urban areas for most of their outdoor investigations will have the best opportunities to compare different plants of this species.

**Salisbury, Sir E.*, Weeds and Aliens (*Collins, 1961*), *page 54.*

The photograph below shows all the leaves from two plants (*X* and *Y*) found growing 6 cm apart in soil that had accumulated in a crack between the base of a wall and the pavement in a Maidstone alleyway. Both were exposed to the same weather conditions.

In this case, therefore, the great difference in the depth of the lobes on the leaves of these two plants cannot be related to differences in environmental conditions. What influence could have been different?

In class discussion about a comparison of this type children might suggest that two seeds from different parent plants had been blown to the same place and produced these two plants. If two offspring are like different parents they could still be unlike each other.

Variation in leaves from two plants of Oxford ragwort

Children in the class can think of some ways in which they are like their parents and then decide which members of the class this makes them unlike.

Can other examples of likenesses between earlier generations and their descendants be found ?

Children could collect information from some of the following sources :

A department of rural studies where some breeding investigations are carried out.
Family photographs.
Parents interested in pigeons, greyhounds or racehorses.
A farmer.
History books (the Habsburg lip ; the illness of the last Tsarevich of Russia).

Does this search provide further evidence for thinking that there may be something that living things can pass on from one generation to another that causes individuals that can be put together in the same set still to remain unlike each other (ie to vary) in certain ways ?

This is about as far as thirteen-year-old children can take these studies. In two or three years' time when they have discovered more about cells and nuclei they will be ready for the investigations that can lead to deeper understanding of variations due to inheritance.

However, teachers need to be continually on guard against the use of expressions that may help to establish inaccurate ideas in children's minds.

When dealing with inheritance it is not correct to speak of *characters* being inherited or passed on from parents to offspring.* What is passed on is genetic material that can combine in many different ways to give the individual receiving it the *capacity for developing* many different characters such as large size, organs of certain shapes or particular colouring.

Even then this inherited potential for developing these characters cannot be fully realised in unfavourable environments which may be created by drought, flooding or lack of sufficient light or suitable food. Here lies the importance of the work of farmers, for instance, who give useful living things the conditions they need for growth and development.

What can we hope children will gain from these early experiences of variation ? Possibly more awareness of the following concepts :

The great number of characters that can vary in living things.
The idea of certain variations being *normally* distributed among groups of individuals.
The possibility of variation increases because of differences in environmental conditions ; or because something passes from parents to their offspring.

Adaptation

One of the most fruitful leading questions children may ask as their experience of variation grows, is whether some of the colours, forms and sizes found in comparable living things are better than others. What is meant by better ?

This will depend on environmental conditions. When moths' wings, for example, match the colour of the bark of trees on which they come to rest, they are much less likely to be visible to predatory birds than similar insects with wings of a darker or lighter colour settling in the same place. Thus in that situation there are advantages in the colour matching the bark. But in another place bark-coloured wings may be conspicuous.

Plants and animals with characters varying in ways that give them some advantage have the best chance of surviving long enough to produce offspring like themselves, while individuals with less useful versions of the same characters are at greater risk of elimination.

A natural process of selection should eventually produce living things with many features well adapted to the conditions prevailing in their habitats (the places where they live) and many parts of the body well adapted to the functions they carry out.

**Huxley, J.*, Evolution (*George Allen and Unwin, 1942*), *page 19.*

Of course, this brief statement is much over-simplified, since the time when children will be sufficiently mature to investigate the many factors, including chance, that influence evolutionary change and adaptation is still some years ahead. Our immediate concern is to help them to continue acquiring the background of early experience that will stand them in good stead when this time comes.

At this stage the experience they need is as much contact as possible with the beautiful and intricate ways in which parts of living things are suited to the jobs they do and to the environment in which they operate. Many of these contacts should be made out of doors where living things in relation to their natural surroundings can be observed.

A number of investigations along these lines have already been suggested, namely:

1. Early reconnaissance in different kinds of places giving children opportunities of asking 'What is it like here?' 'What can live in this kind of place?' (See Volume 2 Part 1, pages 9–11.)

2. Adaptive features in weeds making life in a wide range of environmental conditions possible (See pages 16–20.)

3. Observations and tests likely to provide evidence of relations between form and function. (See pages 31–36.)

4. The study of an animal (or plant) in relation to its surroundings and way of life. (See page 63 for an example of a study of the mole as a burrowing animal.)

Note that children of this age will here be concerned with the external features of the things they examine.

Here children's studies of adaptive features in animals should be concerned with those found in creatures collected locally, for example:

	in relation to	
Earthworm	⟷	life in the soil
Wood louse	⟷	life under stones
Snail	⟷	life in a herbaceous border
Water shrimp or stickleback	⟷	life in a flowing stream
Sparrow or blackbird	⟷	life in an urban area
Caterpillar, chrysalis, butterfly	⟷	life on plants and in the air
Common shore crab or limpet	⟷	life on a rocky shore

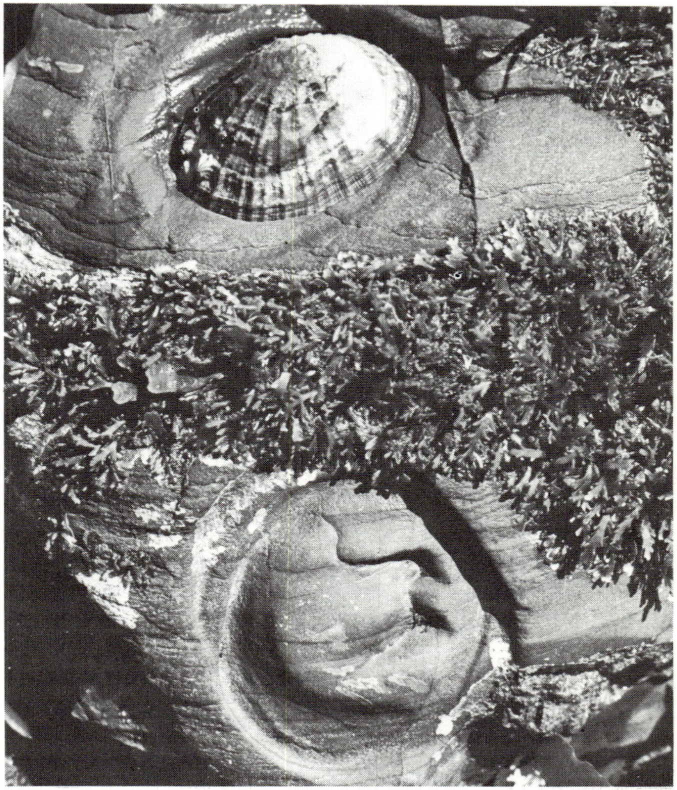
The habitat of the common limpet

Animals in other parts of the world are also very well adapted to their surroundings. However, children are likely to think more actively and frequently about the chrysalids they can measure and compare or the snail with a shell matching the ground on which they themselves can stand, than about passages copied from books about Australian wallabies or North American skunks.

A good project can provide children with further incentives for extending their experience of adaptation, particularly when the theme is one to which they can contribute discoveries made at first hand in the countryside, zoological gardens and museums.

Some suggestions for co-operative investigations

Problem: how do animals avoid danger?

Possible solutions	Out-distancing pursuers	Disguise	Withdrawal to shelter	Resistance or attack
Adaptations to investigate	Long thin legs and digit enlarged to form hoof Claws that grip slippery surfaces when running Streamlined shape	Camouflage by counter-shading and disruptive colouring Imitation Immobility with imitation	Arrangements for sedentary life in tubes or burrows Shells Flattened shape for getting under stones	Spines Stings Poison glands Teeth

The above topic can also be considered from the point of view of the need to capture prey.

Problem: how do animals capture and break up their food?

Possible solutions	Beaks for:	Teeth for:	Tongues for:	Structures for filtering	Mouth parts for:
Adaptations to investigate	Digging Seed cracking Insect capture Straining from water and mud	Gnawing Tearing Grinding	Probing (woodpecker) Lassooing (frog) Scraping (snail)	Gills (molluscs) Tentacles (marine worms)	Biting Sucking Catching (mask of dragon-fly larvae)

Problem: how does pollen reach the stigma of another flower?

Possible solutions	Scattered by wind	Carried by insects
Adaptations to investigate	Size of anthers Way anthers are hinged to filaments Feathery stigmas	Methods of attraction: Massing of small flowers, colour and shape Scent, shape excluding some visitors Methods of protecting pollen from rain Timing: Stamens ripe before pistil Pistil ripe before stamens

Objectives for children learning science

Guide lines to keep in mind

Broad Aims

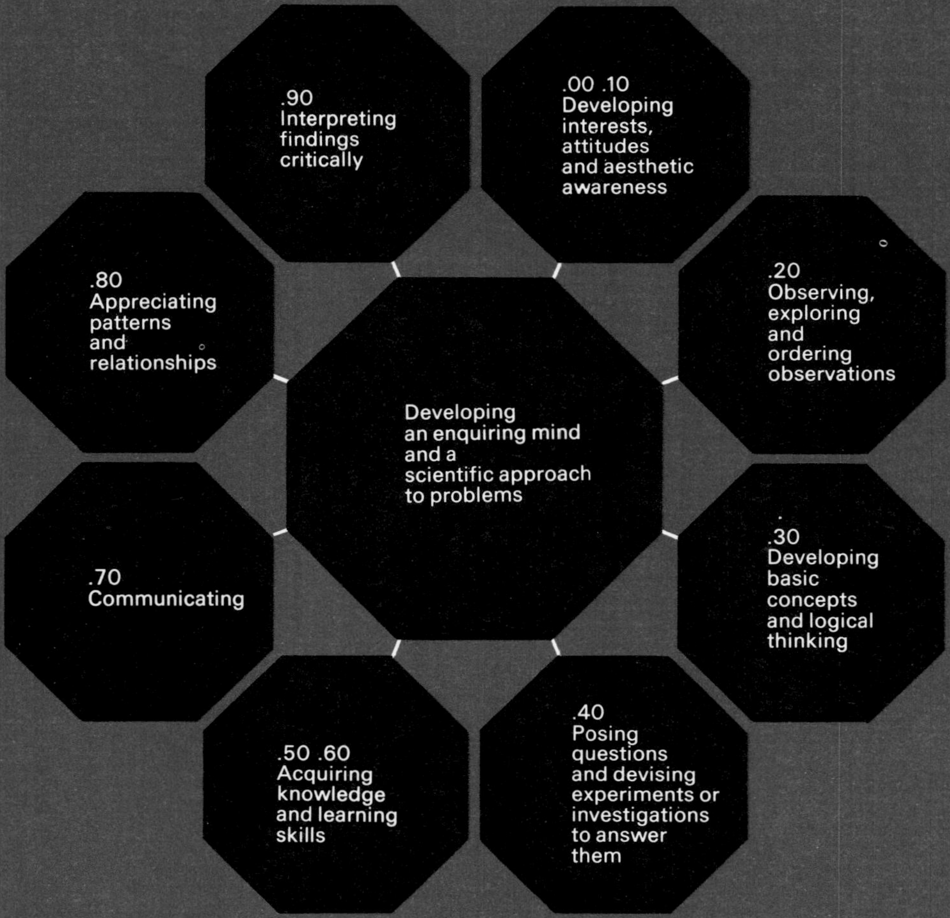

What we mean by Stage 1, Stage 2 and Stage 3

Attitudes, interests and aesthetic awarenes

.00/.10

Stage 1
Transition from intuition to concrete operations. Infants generally.

The characteristics of thought among infant children differ in important respects from those of children over the age of about seven years. Infant thought has been described as 'intuitive' by Piaget; it is closely associated with physical action and is dominated by immediate observation. Generally, the infant is not able to think about or imagine the consequences of an action unless he has actually carried it out, nor is he yet likely to draw logical conclusions from his experiences. At this early stage the objectives are those concerned with active exploration of the immediate environment and the development of ability to discuss and communicate effectively: they relate to the kind of activities that are appropriate to these very young children, and which form an introduction to ways of exploring and of ordering observations.

1.01 Willingness to ask questions
1.02 Willingness to handle both living and non-living material.
1.03 Sensitivity to the need for giving proper care to living things.
1.04 Enjoyment in using all the senses for exploring and discriminating.
1.05 Willingness to collect material for observation or investigation.

Concrete operations. Early stage.

In this Stage, children are developing the ability to manipulate things mentally. At first this ability is limited to objects and materials that can be manipulated concretely, and even then only in a restricted way. The objectives here are concerned with developing these mental operations through exploration of concrete objects and materials—that is to say, objects and materials which, as physical things, have meaning for the child. Since older children, and even adults prefer an introduction to new ideas and problems through concrete example and physical exploration, these objectives are suitable for all children, whatever their age, who are being introduced to certain science activities for the first time.

1.06 Desire to find out things for oneself.
1.07 Willing participation in group work.
1.08 Willing compliance with safety regulations in handling tools and equipment.
1.09 Appreciation of the need to learn the meaning of new words and to use them correctly.

Stage 2
Concrete operations. Later stage.

In this Stage, a continuation of what Piaget calls the stage of concrete operations, the mental manipulations are becoming more varied and powerful. The developing ability to handle variables—for example, in dealing with multiple classification—means that problems can be solved in more ordered and quantitative ways than was previously possible. The objectives begin to be more specific to the exploration of the scientific aspects of the environment rather than to general experience, as previously. These objectives are developments of those of Stage 1 and depend on them for a foundation. They are those thought of as being appropriate for all children who have progressed from Stage 1 and not merely for nine- to eleven-year-olds.

2.01 Willingness to co-operate with others in science activitie
2.02 Willingness to observe objectively.
2.03 Appreciation of the reasons for safety regulations.
2.04 Enjoyment in examining ambiguity in the use of words.
2.05 Interest in choosing suitable means of expressing results and observations.
2.06 Willingness to assume responsibility for the proper care living things.
2.07 Willingness to examine critically the results of their own and others' work.
2.08 Preference for putting ideas to test before accepting or rejecting them.
2.09 Appreciation that approximate methods of comparison m be more appropriate than careful measurements.

Stage 3
Transition to stage of abstract thinking.

This is the Stage in which, for some children, the ability to think about abstractions is developing. When this development is complete their thought is capable of dealing with the possible and hypothetical, and is not tied to the concrete and to the here and now. It may take place between eleven and thirteen for some able children, for some children it may happen later, and for others it may never occur. The objectives of this stage are ones which involve development of ability to use hypothetical reasoning and to separate and combine variables in a systematic way. They are appropriate to those who have achieved most of the Stage 2 objectives and who now show signs of ability to manipulate mentally ideas and propositions.

3.01 Acceptance of responsibility for their own and others' safety in experiments.
3.02 Preference for using words correctly.
3.03 Commitment to the idea of physical cause and effect.
3.04 Recognition of the need to standardise measurements.
3.05 Willingness to examine evidence critically.
3.06 Willingness to consider beforehand the usefulness of the results from a possible experiment.
3.07 Preference for choosing the most appropriate means of expressing results or observations.
3.08 Recognition of the need to acquire new skills.
3.09 Willingness to consider the role of science in everyday li

Attitudes, interests and aesthetic awareness

.00/.10

1.11 Awareness that there are various ways of testing out ideas and making observations.
1.12 Interest in comparing and classifying living or non-living things.
1.13 Enjoyment in comparing measurements with estimates.
1.14 Awareness that there are various ways of expressing results and observations.
1.15 Willingness to wait and to keep records in order to observe change in things.
1.16 Enjoyment in exploring the variety of living things in the environment.
1.17 Interest in discussing and comparing the aesthetic qualities of materials.

2.11 Enjoyment in developing methods for solving problems or testing ideas.
2.12 Appreciation of the part that aesthetic qualities of materials play in determining their use.
2.13 Interest in the way discoveries were made in the past.

3.11 Appreciation of the main principles in the care of living things.
3.12 Willingness to extend methods used in science activities to other fields of experience.

Observing, exploring and ordering observations

.20

1.21 Appreciation of the variety of living things and materials in the environment.
1.22 Awareness of changes which take place as time passes.
1.23 Recognition of common shapes—square, circle, triangle.
1.24 Recognition of regularity in patterns.
1.25 Ability to group things consistently according to chosen or given criteria.

1.26 Awareness of the structure and form of living things.
1.27 Awareness of change of living things and non-living materials.
1.28 Recognition of the action of force
1.29 Ability to group living and non-living things by observable attributes.
1.29a Ability to distinguish regularity in events and motion.

2.21 Awareness of internal structure in living and non-living things.
2.22 Ability to construct and use keys for identification.
2.23 Recognition of similar and congruent shapes.
2.24 Awareness of symmetry in shapes and structures.
2.25 Ability to classify living things and non-living materials in different ways.
2.26 Ability to visualise objects from different angles and the shape of cross-sections.

3.21 Appreciation that classification criteria are arbitrary.
3.22 Ability to distinguish observations which are relevant to the solution of a problem from those which are not.
3.23 Ability to estimate the order of magnitude of physical quantities.

	Developing basic concepts and logical thinking **.30**	Posing questions and devising experiments or investigations to answer them **.40**
Stage 1 Transition from intuition to concrete operations. Infants generally.	*1.31* Awareness of the meaning of words which describe various types of quantity. *1.32* Appreciation that things which are different may have features in common.	*1.41* Ability to find answers to simple problems by investigatic *1.42* Ability to make comparisons in terms of one property or variable.
Concrete operations. Early stage.	*1.33* Ability to predict the effect of certain changes through observation of similar changes. *1.34* Formation of the notions of the horizontal and the vertical. *1.35* Development of concepts of conservation of length and substance. *1.36* Awareness of the meaning of speed and of its relation to distance covered.	*1.43* Appreciation of the need for measurement. *1.44* Awareness that more than one variable may be involved a particular change.
Stage 2 Concrete operations. Later stage.	*2.31* Appreciation of measurement as division into regular parts and repeated comparison with a unit. *2.32* Appreciation that comparisons can be made indirectly by use of an intermediary. *2.33* Development of concepts of conservation of weight, area and volume. *2.34* Appreciation of weight as a downward force. *2.35* Understanding of the speed, time, distance relation.	*2.41* Ability to frame questions likely to be answered through investigations. *2.42* Ability to investigate variables and to discover effective ones. *2.43* Appreciation of the need to control variables and use controls in investigations. *2.44* Ability to choose and use either arbitrary or standard units of measurement as appropriate. *2.45* Ability to select a suitable degree of approximation and work to it. *2.46* Ability to use representational models for investigating problems or relationships.
Stage 3 Transition to stage of abstract thinking.	*3.31* Familiarity with relationships involving velocity, distance, time, acceleration. *3.32* Ability to separate, exclude or combine variables in approaching problems. *3.33* Ability to formulate hypotheses not dependent upon direct observation. *3.34* Ability to extend reasoning beyond the actual to the possible. *3.35* Ability to distinguish a logically sound proof from others less sound.	*3.41* Attempting to identify the essential steps in approaching a problem scientifically. *3.42* Ability to design experiments with effective controls for testing hypotheses. *3.43* Ability to visualise a hypothetical situation as a useful simplification of actual observations. *3.44* Ability to construct scale models for investigation and to appreciate implications of changing the scale.

Acquiring knowledge and learning skills

.50/.60

1.51 Ability to discriminate between different materials.
1.52 Awareness of the characteristics of living things.
1.53 Awareness of properties which materials can have.
1.54 Ability to use displayed reference material for identifying living and non-living things.

1.55 Familiarity with sources of sound.
1.56 Awareness of sources of heat, light and electricity.
1.57 Knowledge that change can be produced in common substances.
1.58 Appreciation that ability to move or cause movement requires energy.
1.59 Knowledge of differences in properties between and within common groups of materials.

2.51 Knowledge of conditions which promote changes in living things and non-living materials.
2.52 Familiarity with a wide range of forces and of ways in which they can be changed.
2.53 Knowledge of sources and simple properties of common forms of energy.
2.54 Knowledge of the origins of common materials.
2.55 Awareness of some discoveries and inventions by famous scientists.
2.56 Knowledge of ways to investigate and measure properties of living things and non-living materials.
2.57 Awareness of changes in the design of measuring instruments and tools during man's history.
2.58 Skill in devising and constructing simple apparatus.
2.59 Ability to select relevant information from books or other reference material.

3.51 Knowledge that chemical change results from interaction.
3.52 Knowledge that energy can be stored and converted in various ways.
3.53 Awareness of the universal nature of gravity.
3.54 Knowledge of the main constituents and variations in the composition of soil and of the earth.
3.55 Knowledge that properties of matter can be explained by reference to its particulate nature.
3.56 Knowledge of certain properties of heat, light, sound, electrical, mechanical and chemical energy.
3.57 Knowledge of a wide range of living organisms.
3.58 Development of the concept of an internal environment.
3.59 Knowledge of the nature and variations in basic life processes.

Acquiring knowledge and learning skills

.50/.60

1.61 Appreciation of man's use of other living things and their products.
1.62 Awareness that man's way of life has changed through the ages.
1.63 Skill in manipulating tools and materials.
1.64 Development of techniques for handling living things correctly.
1.65 Ability to use books for supplementing ideas or information.

3.61 Appreciation of levels of organisation in living things.
3.62 Appreciation of the significance of the work and ideas of some famous scientists.
3.63 Ability to apply relevant knowledge without help of contextual cues.
3.64 Ability to use scientific equipment and instruments for extending the range of human senses.

	Communicating .70	Appreciating patterns and relationships .80
Stage 1 Transition from intuition to concrete operations. Infants generally.	*1.71* Ability to use new words appropriately. *1.72* Ability to record events in their sequences. *1.73* Ability to discuss and record impressions of living and non-living things in the environment. *1.74* Ability to use representational symbols for recording information on charts or block graphs.	*1.81* Awareness of cause-effect relationships.
Concrete operations. Early stage.	*1.75* Ability to tabulate information and use tables. *1.76* Familiarity with names of living things and non-living materials. *1.77* Ability to record impressions by making models, painting or drawing.	*1.82* Development of a concept of environment. *1.83* Formation of a broad idea of variation in living things. *1.84* Awareness of seasonal changes in living things. *1.85* Awareness of differences in physical conditions betwee different parts of the Earth.
Stage 2 Concrete operations. Later stage.	*2.71* Ability to use non-representational symbols in plans, charts, etc. *2.72* Ability to interpret observations in terms of trends and rates of change. *2.73* Ability to use histograms and other simple graphical forms for communicating data. *2.74* Ability to construct models as a means of recording observations.	*2.81* Awareness of sequences of change in natural phenome *2.82* Awareness of structure-function relationship in parts of living things. *2.83* Appreciation of interdependence among living things. *2.84* Awareness of the impact of man's activities on other liv things. *2.85* Awareness of the changes in the physical environment brought about by man's activity. *2.86* Appreciation of the relationships of parts and wholes.
Stage 3 Transition to stage of abstract thinking.	*3.71* Ability to select the graphical form most appropriate to the information being recorded. *3.72* Ability to use three-dimensional models or graphs for recording results. *3.73* Ability to deduce information from graphs: from gradient, area, intercept. *3.74* Ability to use analogies to explain scientific ideas and theories.	*3.81* Recognition that the ratio of volume to surface area is significant. *3.82* Appreciation of the scale of the universe. *3.83* Understanding of the nature and significance of change in living and non-living things. *3.84* Recognition that energy has many forms and is conserv when it is changed from one form to another. *3.85* Recognition of man's impact on living things—conservation, change, control. *3.86* Appreciation of the social implications of man's changi use of materials, historical and contemporary. *3.87* Appreciation of the social implications of research in science. *3.88* Appreciation of the role of science in the changing pattern of provision for human needs.

Interpreting findings critically

.90

1.91 Awareness that the apparent size, shape and relationships of things depend on the position of the observer.

1.92 Appreciation that properties of materials influence their use.

2.91 Appreciation of adaptation to environment.
2.92 Appreciation of how the form and structure of materials relate to their function and properties.
2.93 Awareness that many factors need to be considered when choosing a material for a particular use.
2.94 Recognition of the role of chance in making measurements and experiments.

3.91 Ability to draw from observations conclusions that are unbiased by preconception.
3.92 Willingness to accept factual evidence despite perceptual contradictions.
3.93 Awareness that the degree of accuracy of measurements has to be taken into account when results are interpreted.
3.94 Awareness that unstated assumptions can affect conclusions drawn from argument or experimental results.
3.95 Appreciation of the need to integrate findings into a simplifying generalisation.
3.96 Willingness to check that conclusions are consistent with further evidence.

These Stages we have chosen conform to modern ideas about children's learning. They conveniently describe for us the mental development of children between the ages of five and thirteen years, but it must be remembered that ALTHOUGH CHILDREN GO THROUGH THESE STAGES IN THE SAME ORDER THEY DO NOT GO THROUGH THEM AT THE SAME RATES.
SOME children achieve the later Stages at an early age.
SOME loiter in the early Stages for quite a time.
SOME never have the mental ability to develop to the later Stages.
ALL appear to be ragged in their movement from one Stage to another.
Our Stages, then, are not tied to chronological age, so in any one class of children there will be, almost certainly, some children at differing Stages of mental development.

Index

Ilustration acknowledgements:

The publishers gratefully acknowledge the help given by the following in supplying photographs on the pages indicated:

A-Z Collection, 3, 56 bottom, 57
Heather Angel, 13, 18, 23, 25 left, 27 right, 42, 52, 58, 60, 61, 77
Ardea Photographics, 13 left
C. Ashall, 21
E. P. Hicks, 11
Kentish Gazette, 20
Geoffrey Kinns, 63
Janet Lundie, 2
Mervyn Rees, 27 left, 48
John Topham Limited, 15
P. H. Ward, 28

All other photographs by kind permission of W. H. Petty MA, BSc, County Education Officer, Kent, Photographer: M. Williams

Line drawings by GWA Design Consultants

Cover design by Peter Gauld